THE GLASS SKY

THE GLASS SKY

STORIES OF WOMEN
BREAKING BARRIERS IN THE
OUTDOORS, VERSION 2.0

MARYN CANNON

NEW DEGREE PRESS

THE GLASS SKY

Stories of Women Breaking Barriers in the Outdoors, Version 2.0

ISBN   978-1-64137-114-8   *Paperback*

            978-1-64137-115-5   *Ebook*

To my sisters; may I be like you when I grow up.

CONTENTS

PREFACE TO THE
SECOND EDITION

——

April 2017, Age 21. Yates Field House, Georgetown University. Washington, DC.

Skip, Skip, Pause…no, Skip. Trying to find the perfect song for an uphill climb, I was sitting upright peddling on the spin bike after a long day of class. I take my riding playlist very seriously and usually like to tailor my ride to the progression of songs that feels right in the moment. With the bike set on zero resistance, my legs impatiently cycled around and around underneath me, seemingly moving of their own accord. This springtime Wednesday afternoon, I had been riding for thirty minutes, and although I couldn't seem to find that climbing song, I knew it was time to head up that mountain.

Before I could settle on the right tune, an incoming call from my dad popped up on my screen. It was unusual for him to call me in the middle of the day, so I slowed my legs and my heartbeat, and I answered.

"Hey, Dad, what's up?" I asked.

"Mar, have you heard about REI's new initiative?" he asked excitedly. "They just declared this year 'The Year of the Woman.'"

"No way," I responded in awe. "What does that mean?"

My dad went on to explain the article he had just read and REI's exciting upcoming plans. *The Glass Sky* was published less than ten days prior and I was elated to hear that REI, one of the largest outdoor retailers in the United States, was about to bring the topic of women in the outdoors into the spotlight.

* * *

REI is a national outdoor retail co-op "dedicated to inspiring, educating and outfitting its members and the community for a lifetime of outdoor adventure and stewardship." REI was founded as a member-owned co-op by Mary Anderson in 1938. Mary stayed true to her promise of making high-quality gear accessible for those who needed it most, persevering in a time when women weren't given the opportunity to succeed in business.[1]

REI has continued to innovate over the years and has remained authentically tied to Mary's mentality of "Purpose over Profits." Under the leadership of Jerry Stritzke, REI launched a campaign titled #OptOutside in 2015 that closed the retailer's doors on Black Friday and paid all twelve thousand employees to venture into the wilderness and appreciate time with family outdoors. The campaign was met with significant success, with over 1.4 million people and 170 organizations choosing to #OptOutside. The #OptOutside campaign quickly became a movement. It showcased REI's authentic commitment to their core values, strengthened their brand identity, and galvanized both existing and new stakeholders. They have carried on this tradition for the past two years, and they have built upon their success each year.

Given the scale and influence of their previous #OptOutside campaign, I was excited to see how REI's 2017-2018 #ForceofNature campaign was going to take off. REI has a long history of encouraging female leadership and spreading a spirit of gender equity, and this consumer-facing campaign was built on this foundation of authentic concern as well as new research.

---

1   Staff, REI. "REI History: It Started With An Ice Axe." *REI Co-Op Journal*, REI, 6 Dec. 2016, www.rei.com/blog/camp/rei-history-it-started-with-an-ice-axe.

In a survey of over two thousand women between the ages of eighteen and thirty-five, REI gathered data about the modern woman's relationship with the outdoors. The story their data told is one that is upsetting, albeit not surprising. The good news is that women feel free and liberated from societal pressure in the outdoors, and over 85 percent of the women surveyed believe that being outdoors positively affects mental health, physical health, happiness, and overall well-being. The disappointing news is that six out of every ten women voiced that men are taken more seriously than women in the outdoors, and six out of ten also were unable to think of an outdoor female role model when prompted.[2]

The contradictory relationship between these aforementioned conclusions showed REI that there is significant opportunity to improve the experience of the modern woman in the outdoors. They set out with a four-step plan to make tangible change in the industry. They committed to changing the narrative, creating a strong community, closing the gear gap, and investing in communities passionate about advancing women in the outdoors.

To achieve these goals, they pledged to share the stories of the women that are in the outdoors, doing it. They also committed to executing over one thousand events for women around

2   REI. "2017 National Study on Women and the Outdoors." LinkedIn SlideShare, REI, 30 Mar. 2017, www.slideshare.net/REI_/2017-national-study-on-women-and-the-outdoors.

the country and adding more sizes and options for women's gear. Lastly, they created the Force of Nature Fund, a fund that pledged to invest over one million dollars in programs that create opportunities for girls and women in the outdoors. This multi-pronged approach was aimed at encouraging female trailblazers and rule breakers to recognize their own value and place in the outdoors and encourage other women to do the same.[3]

* * *

Sitting on the bike that Wednesday afternoon, I knew I was going to learn a lot more about women in the outdoor industry in the upcoming year. I was excited to follow the Force of Nature conversation and hear more stories from women who are kicking butt in the outdoors. I'm pleased to say that I learned even more than I predicted and one year later, *The Glass Sky* needs updating.

I initially set out to write a book about how a woman should break into the outdoor industry—sharing the stories of several women who have successfully done so and documenting learnings from their experience. One year later, I've decided to make some changes to my thesis. Rather than tell a reader *how she should* break into the outdoor industry, I tell a reader *why* she should break into the outdoor industry.

---

3   REI. "Force of Nature." REI, www.rei.com/h/force-of-nature.

This change is necessary for a few reasons. The first is that women are told all day, every day what they *should* do and how they *should* behave. Thus in hindsight, it seems somewhat contradictory that a book focused on female empowerment emphasize what a woman should and shouldn't do. It doesn't seem appropriate that a book focused on female strength take the form of a "how to."

The second is that the previous message of this book was sneakily, yet inherently, flawed. The message was flawed because there is no definitive recipe for "how to" successfully break into the outdoor industry—for two reasons. First, every woman exists within a unique context, and thus "successfully breaking into the outdoor industry" cannot be universally defined. For some, success means securing that dream job as an outdoor education instructor. For others, it means carving out twenty minutes before a busy workday to go for a hike, and still for others, it means winning an Olympic gold on the slopes. The second reason this message is flawed is that even if we were to [erroneously] select one definition for what it means to be "successful" in the outdoors, there is no way to describe or predict the path that will lead to that success. It would be impossible to outline the specific actions a woman should take to reach that success, as successful outdoorswomen have had vastly different journeys. It's unreasonable to emphasize one journey as universally advisable.

Looking back at the stories I collected, I saw that these anecdotes share less about *how* a woman should get outside and more about *why* a woman should get outside. They point to the challenges and rewards that are unique to women in the outdoors, and they offer inspiration to all women, regardless of their current relationship with the outdoors.

In reworking this second edition, I aim to tell of the challenges and rewards women uniquely face from being outside and making the outdoors a part of their life. Through sharing my journey and the journeys of inspirational women, I hope to create a narrative that leaves the reader feeling inspired and itching to get outside. I hope this book communicates that she is part of a larger community that is coming together to empower women of all backgrounds to pursue outdoor activity.

INTRODUCTION

July 2016, Age 20. Trans-Canada Highway Ontario, Canada.

I dug around for my shoes in the pile of sweatshirts, granola bar wrappers, and water bottles that had accumulated during our six-hour drive. I spotted them underneath Katie, our dog, who had found a comfortable spot wedged between the bags of groceries at my feet. Seeing how soundly Katie was sleeping, I questioned how much I really needed my shoes. We were nearing Coffee Time, the last food establishment for miles, and though we were only about thirty minutes from our destination, we had to stop for doughnut holes. The sound of the pouring rain hitting the roof of our car brought me back to reality and I gently shook Katie awake. Coffee Time makes the best doughnut holes in Canada, and tradition is tradition. If you ever find yourself in Ontario driving along

Country Road 28, I highly recommend you stop into this cash-only doughnut mecca.

I slipped my sneakers on clog-style and used the luggage sitting next to me to launch myself out the side door of our Jeep. I stretched my arms over my head, soaking in the hot and humid June rain. My sister, Terese, brought Katie's leash around the car and coaxed the sleepy dog out for a rainy bathroom break.

Our feet crunched on the wet gravel as my younger sister, Hannah, and I made our way into Coffee Time. Besides the scrumptious doughnuts, Coffee Time offered us one last opportunity to access a flushing toilet before we reached our lake house that sits on an island and lacks electricity and modern plumbing. I've always had a certain fondness for our double-seater outhouse—the views certainly beat those offered in the dimly lit Coffee Time stall—but I've always appreciated one last opportunity to wash my hands with hot running water before we reach the lake.

Hannah placed our regular order as I relieved myself. We returned to the car a few minutes later and took Katie off of Terese's hands so that she too could take advantage of the facilities. I corralled Katie into the backseat and cringed as she shook her wet fur. When she had finished, I jumped in after her, unsuccessfully trying to steer her clear of our dry clothes that littered the back seat. Five minutes later, we were back on the road, country music blasting and windshield wipers whipping, headed toward Stony Lake.

After nine more Taylor Swift songs, we reached the end of that short and scenic final stretch. We turned off the paved road and onto the dirt road that leads to Kawartha Park Marina. Despite the rain, Katie immediately smelled the distinctive lake air, and she began to whimper with excitement, scampering from window to window. At the end of the two-mile road, our Jeep rolled to a stop outside the marina.

"Well, I hoped it was going to stop raining," Terese said, turning the key and zipping up her rain jacket, "but I brought some bags and we'll make do."

"I'll start bagging," Hannah said with a sigh. "I need the tunes on though."

"Of course, of course," Terese laughed as she brought the car back to life and turned up the volume.

Our lake house is a fifteen-minute boat ride from the marina (sometimes longer, depending on how many people are there to weigh down the boat). Getting ourselves and all our stuff to the cottage in the rain is a laborious process and often results in a few days' worth of wet clothing. Wet clothing poses a real inconvenience, as we rely on the clothesline to dry our clothes. When rain is persistent, we run out of dry clothing quickly. Luckily, Terese had thought ahead and packed a box of garbage bags, just in case we found ourselves in this situation.

I took off Katie's collar as she scratched and whined at the window and opened the door for her. She sprang into freedom, splashing through the puddles as she made her rounds at full speed to the chorus of Taylor Swift's "Love Story." I smiled as I watched her go. At that moment she was easily the happiest dog on Earth.

I pulled on my hood and hopped out to help Hannah cover our food, backpacks, and duffels with garbage bags while Terese ran down the docks to bail the tin motorboat our grandma had dropped off for us the night before. I felt grateful to be on garbage bag duty as I watched Terese stand on the stern of the boat and start bailing with our old Folgers tin. I stood up on my tiptoes, squinting through the rain in an attempt to gauge how much water we were dealing with. I grimaced— there had to be over a hundred gallons in there. It looked like it had been coming down all night.

After about half an hour, we pushed off and started our long but happy journey to the cottage. Hannah sat in the back, fighting the old warped tiller motor with one hand and shielding her eyes from the intense rainfall with the other. We each knew this lake like the back of our hand, but it was good to have eyes looking ahead for rocks, especially on a dark day like today. Although the journey was slow given the food and clothes that we had piled between the thwarts, morale was high.

In the rain, the lake somehow felt more majestic. A wave of gratitude and reverence washed over me as we passed between the Sister Islands. The sisters are two striking granite islands that face each other; the "Big Sister" flat and long, the "Little Sister" mountainous and smaller. They're intricately spotted with bright green moss and a few tall and imposing pine trees. Despite the rain, I could still see the fire pit on the Little Sister where we climb up to roast marshmallows at the end of every summer. No matter what had happened over the past year, there was something deeply comforting about returning to this place that didn't change. It felt like coming home.

Several minutes later, we turned around Turner's Island, and our own little island came into view. On it stands our lake house, "The Shanty." The Shanty was originally built as a hunting lodge in 1806 and somehow our family found their way up here and fell in love with it seven generations ago. Hannah slowed the boat as we entered the inlet and neared the dock. Before she was able to park, Katie leaped from the boat and soared over the five-foot gap, her front paws hitting the old dock with a loud thump. We laughed and cheered her on as she shook her fur and paraded around proudly, waiting for us non-risk-takers to land at the dock.

We tied up the boat and began hauling our things up the crooked wooden stairs that connect the dock to the island. I'm always careful trudging up those stairs, as I keenly remember slipping off the stairs and into the thin slice of water between the dock and the rock as a little kid. We unpacked our clothes and filled the propane fridge, feeling grateful that our garbage bags had done the trick. After peeling off our soaking clothes, we threw on our swimsuits. Rain or no rain, it was a race to be the first to jump off the diving board. That first splash always felt the sweetest.

* * *

October 2016, Age 21. Alumni Square Apartments, Georgetown University. Washington, DC.

I opened my eyes wide and blinked rapidly a few times, trying to wake myself up. I had just taken a brief post-dinner nap, something I hadn't done since I had the flu in high school. It was only Tuesday, but it felt like it should be a Friday. Midterms had started this week, and I had already had two exams: one yesterday in Economics, and one this morning in Business Statistics. Despite my power nap, I felt pretty wiped as I sat down at my desk and prepared to make a call to Kate Taylor, one of the best fly fishers in the world.

As soon as the clock hit 8 p.m., I plugged in her Oregon area code and dialed her number. I listened to six rings before I heard a pleasant "Hello?"

"Hi, Kate!" I said, "This is Maryn Cannon, calling to interview you…we spoke over email last week."

"Oh, hi!" she responded. "I'm happy you caught me, I completely forgot!"

I smiled widely. I think we would be friends. We chatted for about six seconds before the connection started acting funky.

"I'm sorry. I'm driving through a windstorm in Alaska, and I don't think the connection will last much longer…" she said.

"Oh, no worries!" I replied, tipping back on the hind legs of my chair. I began to hear a soft static and pulled my phone away from my ear as I hovered. I heard a loud click, and we were promptly disconnected.

I leaned forward, the levitating legs of my chair hitting the floor with a loud thump. I let out a heavy sigh, looked at the black screen and placed my phone on the desk. Leaning back, I sank down in my chair and looked up at my white dorm room ceiling. I felt discouraged that I wasn't able to interview Kate since I had read extensively about her successes and was excited to hear about her journey. I soon realized that more than discouraged, I felt refreshed. It was exciting to envision the wild weather up north. It made me yearn for our summer adventures in Canada. I had felt a wave of second-hand adrenaline and excitement imagining myself driving beside her, braving the unpredictable Alaskan elements.

"A windstorm in Alaska…" I thought, "that feels so far away. So far away from my desk piled with textbooks and the flickering fluorescent light above my head." I looked up at the wavering light, squinting my eyes, "I'd like to be driving through a windstorm in Alaska."

* * *

My twelve-second conversation with Kate Taylor convinced me to sit down and write this book. While we go about our daily routine, women around the world are accomplishing amazing feats in the outdoors. These feats vary significantly and range from driving through a windstorm in Alaska to getting out of the house and going for a hike after a long day at work. Something needs to be said about these women who are kicking butt in the outdoors. These women are all around us. We are these women.

* * *

There was a steep hill in one of the fields about a quarter mile from the house where I grew up. My sisters and I spent each fall rolling down that hill into a pile of crisp red leaves we had raked together at the bottom. During the winters, we sledded down that hill on beat-up plastic saucers that smacked the ice and threw us off (laughing hysterically) more often than not. And in the springtime, we tripped down that same hill, chasing our kite in the crisp April air. We would shout and jump when our kite had "lift-off," and we would run for hours if that meant we could keep it flying.

Now a third-year student in college living far away from that hill and our family house on the lake, I contemplate my future career and lifestyle. This book was developed as I stand at this crossroads. The road to the left is clean, well-paved and lined with bright street lights while the road to the right is sketchy, unpaved, and pitch black. It would be easy to pick the road on the left—the traditional career path. It appears to be safe and comfortable. This is what I am supposed to do. But something keeps me from falling into step with the hundreds of my peers that have chosen this path. The alternative seems unfamiliar and risky, but I am curious. I am curious about what an "alternative" job in the outdoor industry would look like, and if there is another, third, path that incorporates a traditional career and simultaneous dedication to and committed participation in outdoor recreation.

In October of 2017, I made an appointment with one of our university's esteemed career coaches. After brief introductions and a series of questions pertaining to my academic and extracurricular interests, my career coach listed a series of steps she commonly suggests to students in the job search process. We began to run through them together, starting with the first question: What industries are you drawn to?

"I am drawn to the Outdoor Industry," I replied, excitedly.

As she had with my previous answers, she quickly scribbled my answer on her legal pad. This time, however, she paused and left her pen pressed on the paper at the end of the line. Brow furrowed, she looked up at me and clicked her pen shut, resting it on the yellow page in front of her.

"Did you know," she started, "I have been working as a collegiate career coach for over thirty years… and no student has ever answered 'The Outdoor Industry'?"

* * *

More than 142 million Americans participated in an outdoor activity at least once in 2015. Over $646 billion of their hard-earned money was spent on that outdoor recreation. This big-spending supports over 6.1 million direct jobs and generates over $80 billion in federal, state, and local tax revenue.

The Outdoor Industry is an overlooked economic giant and will likely continue to grow in the coming years.[4] These numbers show that we should care about the Outdoor Industry.

For the average college student, there is no talk about how to make a living in the Outdoor Industry; there are no recruiting sessions for adventuring. Significant focus is placed on professional development and career exploration, but it has been my experience that this discussion often fails to address the "passion path" and the value of exploring outdoor interests in conjunction with professional (and traditional) work. I am grateful for the overwhelmingly expansive array of resources that have helped me search for a traditional job, but I have still been left unsatisfied.

When I imagined a typical employee in the Outdoor Industry, I pictured a tall, bearded man. He was wearing a red flannel shirt and tattered work boots. He looked strong and capable, and he became strong from hours of labor in the outdoors. He hadn't spent much time in the gym.

I have always seen myself as strong and able. And although I am confident in that fact, there has always been a little voice in my head that questions whether I possess the traits that are a necessary to take a job or pursue my passion in the outdoors.

---

4   "Outdoor Participation Report 2016." Outdoor Industry Association, The Outdoor Foundation, outdoorindustry.org/resource/outdoor-participation-report-2016/.

What qualities are required for a female to achieve success in an outdoor profession? Moreover, if a woman pursues a profession in a different industry, what opportunities does she have to simultaneously pursue her passion for the outdoors? In other words, what does the modern female's experience look like in the outdoors?

This book aims to showcase inspirational women who model success in the outdoors. Their vast array of experiences show that success means something different for every woman. For some, success means they have found a job in the outdoor industry (either in the athletic or corporate sphere), and for others, it simply means they have found a way to incorporate their love of the outdoors into their busy lives. Taken together, these stories show why more women should get outside. Some of these inspirational figures include:

- One of most skilled fly-fishing guides in North America
- The Vice President of United States Sailing and member of the 1988 US Olympic Team
- The gold medal winner in Slopestyle Snowboarding Event, 2014 Winter Olympics
- One of the most talented professional alpine climbers in the world
- An ultramarathon runner and long-distance backpacker
- A professional kite surfer

- A Volvo Ocean Race sailor and United States Team sailor for 10+ years
- One of the most skilled professional kayakers in the world
- A professional skier and international ski coach
- An outdoor education instructor and solo-backpacker
- The former president and CEO of CamelBak, former Vice President of The North Face
- And so many more…

All of these experts are badass women (like we'd all probably like to be). They shared their stories and why they couldn't imagine doing anything else. These women have taught me about what it is like to be a female in the modern Outdoor Industry. The female's experience is uniquely marked by gender bias and even the most badass female athletes in outdoor sports frequently experience unwarranted prejudice.

Admittedly, this issue of gender bias and discrimination spans all industries in today's modern society. We've heard this story before, but what is unique about the Outdoor Industry is that this gender bias is one that is rarely challenged. Gender bias in the outdoors doesn't seem to be studied or challenged as frequently as gender bias in other industries because this bias has been justified on the surface level by the male's strength advantage and his traditional masculine traits that allegedly lead to success in the outdoors.

Change is coming, as many strong women and men are working to empower women in the outdoors. Time in the outdoors has incredible value to all women—regardless of their past experiences and skill level. So, who's ready for that windstorm?

PART 1

WHY

The wilderness holds answers to questions
[WOMAN] has not yet learned to ask.

—NANCY NEWHALL

PART 1

WHY

1

WHY DO WE CARE?

———

July 2017, Age 21. Interstate 110 North, Los Angeles, California

I put the car in park, turned off the air conditioning and rolled down the windows. I lifted up my legs and stretched my feet, cringing as I peeled my thighs one by one from the black leather. It felt like ripping off a Band-Aid—unpleasant but satisfying. I scooted my butt backward in the driver's seat and reluctantly relaxed back into the pools of sweat that had gathered underneath my quads. My hand hovered over the gear shift, but glancing up at the parking lot in front of me, I stretched my arms and put my hands behind my head instead. It was rush hour on the 110—I knew I would be stopped here for a while.

* * *

After six weeks of making the daily commute from South Los Angeles to Redondo Beach, I had developed a love-hate relationship with the I-110. I loved it some days because it offered uninterrupted thinking time and I hated it on others for the same reason. I know they say the most successful people spend their commute time learning from podcasts or listening to audiobooks, but I tried that and it didn't stick. I much preferred sitting back and listening to my Spotify on shuffle. Traffic was stop-and-go, and although it only took me about an hour (on average) to reach my destination, it often felt like longer—especially on the way home.

I found myself in California by chance. I had responded to a career posting on our campus website on a whim and ended up taking a summer internship at a small publishing company in Redondo Beach. I had been hearing about the importance of the post-junior year internship for months, but truth be told I didn't pay much attention to the job itself. I was most excited about moving to California to live with my twin sister, Terese. Terese plays beach volleyball for USC and stays in California over the summer to train. I jumped at the opportunity to spend one more summer as her roommate.

As the summer began to unfold, I realized that I had over-romanticized my summer plans. While it was exciting to be living with Terese, most days she was busy training late into the evening and she ended up traveling on the pro tour for six of the ten weeks I was there. Similarly, while it was cool to have the opportunity to explore a new city, LA isn't as easily navigable as I assumed it would be, and after a full workday, I lacked the motivation to get out and drive another hour and a half to get to a tourist destination. Far from home, I found it difficult to make friends. I spent my days working in an eight-person office and my nights sitting on the couch in an eerily empty college neighborhood. I wasn't feeling like myself. In one of the "most happening" cities in the country, I felt lonely.

* * *

I sang as I drove along the I-110 that Friday afternoon. I had been looking forward to this weekend for the past few weeks because Terese had Saturday off. She was playing in a local one-day beach volleyball tournament on Sunday, which meant that for the first time in weeks, she was in town and had a free Saturday. She had agreed to go on a hike with me. To celebrate, I made a pit stop at Trader Joe's to pick up some chocolate peanut butter cups (our favorite) for that night's dessert. Still parked on the freeway, I eyed the chocolates as they rested innocently on the dashboard, tempting me. I reached out to them, but before I could break into the package, the cars in front of me began to creep forward.

"That was probably for the best," I thought with a sigh, assessing how melted they were, "We need to get those bad boys in the fridge." I dropped the chocolate back on the dash and cranked the car into drive. For the next ten miles, I rolled along slowly with the rest of the commuters, enjoying the ABBA soundtrack as I saw and felt the heat waves rise from the pavement outside my window. I couldn't bring myself to turn on the air conditioning, even as I watched the chocolate melt. I was enjoying the gentle highway breeze floating across my face.

Forty minutes later, I pulled into our driveway. On those rare days when Terese was in town, coming home was my favorite part of the day. Glancing at the screen door, I turned the music all the way up, letting "Dancing Queen" ring out for anyone within a quarter mile to hear. "You're welcome, South Central," I thought as I raised my voice to sing along. Terese busted out onto the porch, sliding in her socks. She skidded to a stop with a huge smile on her face just in time for the refrain and I leaped out of the car, leaving my door open so we could hear the music at full volume. We danced our way through the next two songs, much to our delight and our neighbors' chagrin. After the woman next door closed her kitchen window with a bang, we decided to bring our party inside.

We went to bed early that night, full of chocolate peanut butter cups and excited for our upcoming adventure. We didn't know exactly where we were going, but I had researched several hiking destinations and we picked one at random over dinner. It was called Stunt Road Trail, and it was only about an hour away.

The next morning, I woke up early and excited to get the day going. I loaded my backpack with two PB&Js, some Luna bars, and two full Nalgenes. We hit the road, and after a few unintentional detours (navigation has never been my strong suit), we found our way to a dirt path with a small dilapidated sign that read "Stunt Rd." Terese looked at me, an amused grin spreading across her face. With a barely perceptible shrug, she turned the wheel and we began to roll down the winding off-road path. Having no idea where we were, we parked where we saw another car pulled over and hopped out.

We followed the path that led into the woods, doing our best to memorize the defining characteristics of that entrance so that we might also use it as an exit. Ten minutes into our adventure, I felt a wave of relaxation come over me. Climbing up the steep and sandy ascent, drenched in sweat and covered in sand, my calves screamed and my backpack felt like it was stuffed with bricks. Small signs posted every ten feet informed us that we were entering rattlesnake territory. Neither of us had ever seen a rattlesnake before and although the idea of encountering one did not sound pleasant, we pushed on. As we moved, we fell into a rhythm. Our rhythm was by no means comfortable, as we were focused on getting to the top and pushed the pace accordingly. Our conversation slowly faded and the only noise that disrupted nature's silence was our heavy breathing and the sound of my heartbeat in my ears. For the first time in weeks, I felt present.

About thirty minutes in, we reached a paved road crossing. We paused for the first time that day and I looked at Terese, laughing as she peeped under the brim of her baseball hat and wiped the sweat that was dripping down her face with the back of my hand.

"Is my Division 1 NCAA National Champion sister a little bit out of breath?" I teased as I passed her a water bottle for a swig.

"Yeah, yeah" she smiled, poking my ribs and causing me to spit out a full mouth of water, "Let's keep going."

As we continued our ascent, I felt my worries about making friends and finding my place fall off my shoulders, and I felt my homesickness dissipate in the dust we kicked up behind us. Surrounded by big green foliage and tall brown mountains, I felt small and my troubles felt small. As I felt the sunshine beating down on my shoulders I was overwhelmed with a deep sense of gratitude for this day. I felt more like myself than I had in the past six weeks.

* * *

At some of the most pivotal moments in my life, time in the outdoors has completely altered my perspective. In those times when I have felt an unrelenting sadness, loneliness, or confusion I have found what I needed—no matter what that ended up being—in the outdoors. I rarely went outside with the intention to seek solutions to my problems; I rarely went outside with the self-realization that I was feeling lost and was in need of healing. However, reflecting back on my relationship with the outdoors, I can see a clear pattern where my time in the outdoors has offered me a genuine sense of comfort and a refreshing sense of clarity in the moments when I needed it most.

When I was a sophomore in high school, I went through a period of sadness that I couldn't seem to shake. In the dead of winter, my parents piled on the layers and whisked me off to a local trail for a day hike. I finished the hike that day with a refreshed perspective and the realization that I needed to find a new and challenging activity outside of school and outside of sports. I was at a loss for what that activity might be, but after our hike, my dad drove us to a local bakery to warm up with a hot chocolate. Feeling like I could take on the world, I asked for an application. I worked at that bakery for the next four years, and it played a huge part in shaping who I am today. I don't know if I would have found my way to that special spot without that time in the woods.

As a college student, I did a summer study abroad program in Spain. After about a month, I began to feel homesick. One afternoon, I realized I needed to get off of campus and decided to follow a trail behind our dorm building. I had sat on my bed and watched hikers emerge from that trail for the past few weeks, so deeming it safe, I laced up my sneakers and set off along the dirt path. I followed the path, not knowing where I was headed, but enjoying the view. I ran through open fields into a heavily wooded area, densely packed with tall leafy trees. About an hour into my trip, I felt the sky begin to darken and I realized I needed to turn around. Pausing to look up at the beautiful foreign vegetation all around me, I was hit with the realization of just how lucky I was to be studying in a European country. I had spent my whole life dreaming of traveling and exploring the world, and here I was running on a Spanish trail, traveling and exploring the world. I ran back to my dorm with a new bounce in my step, promising myself that I wouldn't take my remaining time for granted.

* * *

Researchers have discovered that spending time outside offers significant benefits to a person's well-being. Being outside strengthens your mental health, seeing as walking outside is strongly linked to lower rates of depression and stress. According to studies done by Happify, when we're outside, our bodies "produce lower levels of pro-inflammatory cytokines, thereby promoting a healthier state of mind. Aside from creating a positive frame of mind, being in touch with nature helps boost our serotonin (the feel-good neurotransmitter in our bodies) levels." What's more, it also increases activity in parts of the brain that are linked to empathy, emotional stability, and love.[5]

Moreover, REI's recent nationwide survey found that more than 85 percent of women believe the outdoors positively affects mental health, physical health, happiness, and overall well-being. Additionally, seven in ten women feel they are under more pressure to conform than men, and the outdoors provides an escape from this stress, as 72 percent of women report that they feel liberated or free when they are outdoors, and 74 percent of women assert that the outdoors is a place to escape the stresses of everyday life. Overall, the survey found that time outdoors equals happiness.[6]

Although women are positioned to uniquely benefit from time in the outdoors, they are less likely to spend time outdoors for a variety of reasons including a lack of accessibility and sense of belonging and community in the outdoors. Many strong and inspiring women have made it their livelihood to put an end to this unjust and disconcerting contradiction. They have found along the way that time spent in the outdoors not only

5   Chang, Angel. "Spending Time Outdoors Will Improve Your Health In 9 Fascinating Ways."LittleThings.com, 17 Nov. 2015, www.littlethings.com/benefits-of-being-outside/.

6   REI. "2017 National Study on Women and the Outdoors." LinkedIn SlideShare, REI, 30 Mar. 2017, www.slideshare.net/REI_/2017-national-study-on-women-and-the-outdoors.

increases happiness; in many cases, it empowers women to overcome significant life challenges.

One of these women is Elise Knicely, founder of She is ABLE, an Atlanta-based nonprofit that offers outdoor experiences and trips for marginalized women—specifically women that have been victims of abuse. In a recent interview with the *Misadventures* magazine, she pointed out that "doctors and therapists are now offering 'being outside' as a treatment plan for people with anxiety, depression, and other disorders. It's also no new news that being outside helps people clear their heads, get their daily dose of Vitamin D, and lift energy level and moods…Many of our participants have experienced neglect, abuse and severe trauma…At She Is ABLE, we make it our mission to encourage and challenge our participants to reconnect with their physical self in order to seek deeper emotional healing and liberation. A powerful thing happens when a woman sees her body as not just a tool for abuse and neglect, but as a powerful, capable, and strong. That mental shift leads to such strong feelings of self-worth and accomplishment, and man, we love that!"[7]

Another female founder, Traci Saor, established a nonprofit organization called G.O.N.E about five years ago. G.O.N.E. is dedicated to helping women in domestic violence situations

---

7   "Interview: Elise Knicely // She Is ABLE | Misadventures." Misadventures Magazine, Misadventures, 17 May 2017, misadventuresmag.com/interview-elise-knicely-able/.

find empowerment in the outdoors. Traci has felt and seen the benefits of time spent outdoors firsthand, saying: "Once you conquer your fear of bugs, wildlife, paddling on deep water, or of learning new things, it becomes easier for you to conquer that fear of leaving the abusive situation, conquer the fear of applying for a job, moving your children, or starting a new life."[8]

The Outdoor Women's Alliance wrote an article on the organization, saying: "When women go on a trip with G.O.N.E., they experience a one-on-one connection between past victims who know the power of the outdoors to restore life and current victims who may think life is not worth living. It's loosely run. There's no schedule, no hotline, no 501 nonprofit status. It's staffed only by volunteer labor, operates with used gear, and is advertised by word of mouth. We contact local shelters to see if there are any women interested in an outing. Quick paddles or overnight camping might happen at a moment's notice. We load gear, pick up our guest, and head out for an afternoon or a weekend, whatever weather and schedules allow. In a criticism-free environment, the women are at liberty to speak about their past, share their pain, and begin to move past it. As the group paddles or walks, the women start to heal and find peace. As Danielle put it after the trip,

---

8   Malordy, Jessica C. "Traci Saor: Founder of G.O.N.E. | Misadventures." Misadventures Magazine, 19 Jan. 2017, misadventuresmag.com/traci-saor-founder-of-g-o-n-e/.

'I could finally breathe.'"[9]

Time in the outdoors not only has mental and emotional benefits, it also has pronounced physical benefits. The Canadian Association for the Advancement of Women and Sport and Physical Activity recently published a detailed list of benefits that stem from general female involvement in sports. Their findings show that females feel physical health benefits, psychological and emotional benefits, and social and cultural benefits. The physical health benefits range from cardiorespiratory fitness and overall bone health to healthy menstrual function. Research shows that these physical health benefits are so great that they lead to a longer and better quality of life. Emotional benefits include empowerment, optimal cognitive functioning, and decreased levels of anxiety, depression, and neuroticism. Several social benefits include positive gender construction, healthy body image, and risk behavior reduction.[10]

I can attest to these benefits, as I have felt them through my own outdoor experiences. It is clear that no matter a woman's current situation, there are significant mental, emotional, and physical benefits of getting outside and being active. And it's important we remember that to feel these positive effects of

9   Malordy, Jessica C. "Traci Saor: Founder of G.O.N.E. | Misadventures." Misadventures Magazine, 19 Jan. 2017, misadventuresmag.com/traci-saor-founder-of-g-o-n-e/.

10 Johnstone, Lori, and Sydney Millar. "Actively Engaging Women and Girls." 2012.

nature, we don't have to climb the highest peak in the country—often simply going for a walk in our neighborhood can
refresh and restart our day. No matter our experience-level
or our surroundings, it's in our own best interest to actively
seek time in the outdoors and make outdoor activity a routine
part of our life.

2

WHICH WOMEN ARE WE TALKING ABOUT?

———

November 2016, Age 21. Intercultural Center, Georgetown University, Washington, DC.

It had been awhile since I had visited Professor Park's office, but I knew what building it was in so I decided to wing it. After fruitlessly and somewhat desperately searching for her door for twenty minutes, I checked my watch and realized I was officially late. Heart pounding, I barreled up the stairs to the fifth (and highest) floor. I had tried every floor but the fifth. A huge smile spread across my face when I emerged from the stairwell to find "Professor Park, *Women and Gender Studies*" written on the first door I saw. Whoops.

I knocked softly on the office door and found her reading peacefully at her desk. I sank into her leather couch with a single bead of sweat running down my temple and apologized for my lateness. After our initial greetings, I launched into the outline of my book topic. If I remember correctly, I spoke with a lot of excitement and perhaps too many hand motions. She listened patiently, scribbling little notes on her desk pad. When I had finished, I sat back, anxiously awaiting her reaction.

Professor Park took off her glasses and swiveled her chair so that she was fully facing me. Looking directly into my eyes, she asked: "What women are you talking about?"

"All women…" I responded immediately but somewhat tentatively. "Yes, I think all women," I said with slightly more confidence.

"How is that so?" she asked.

I furrowed my brow and leaned forward. Chin in my palm, I scraped the back of my brain in an attempt to find an answer to this seemingly simple yet extremely difficult question. The real answer was that I had not yet considered what women I was writing about. I had not yet considered how the other aspects of a woman's identity play into her outdoor experience.

I had some explaining to do.

"Outdoor activity is inevitably and necessarily a classed and racial phenomenon." She began. "This intersectionality might be important to include in your research, even if you don't decide to include it in your book." She said, placing her pen on her pad. "It is impossible to write about the experience of all women."

"You are so right," I said thoughtfully. The truth of her words hit me pretty hard. I realized in that moment how ignorant I had been in my research, and unknowingly simplistic in my claims. I felt disappointed in myself.

* * *

According to the most recent "In-Depth-Look" of the female outdoor recreation population released by the Outdoor Industry Association, the average female outdoor recreation participant is age thrity-seven, married (53 percent), Caucasian (80 percent), and earns 53-57K a year. This data points to a significant trend within the female outdoor population. Impoverished women and women of color make up only a small percentage of our national female outdoor participants.

When I read these statistics, I was surprised and somewhat alarmed. It occurred to me then that the majority of the women I interviewed were Caucasian—these women were on the list of well-known names that surfaced in my research. It makes sense, upon reflection, that women who have become well-known in the outdoor community might have had privileges that other women have not. Access to outdoor activity often is dependent on a person's location, leisure time, and financial freedom. Many women are simply not introduced to outdoor sport because their families do not have the ability to or the interest in providing that access to them. Access to the outdoors requires more than a will to simply get outside, and for some, the sacrifices seem too big to justify.

The Outdoor Industry's 2016 Participation report reflects the fact that these privileges play a role in outdoor participation as a whole. In 2016, 62 percent of outdoor participants had at least one year of college education, and 65 percent report an annual income of over $50,000. Additionally, 74 percent of participants are white, 9 percent are African American, 8 percent are Hispanic, and 7 percent are Asian/Pacific Islander.

According to Google Dictionary, intersectionality is defined as: "the interconnected nature of social categorizations such as race, class, and gender as they apply to a given individual or group, regarded as creating overlapping and interdependent systems of discrimination or disadvantage."[11] These statistics show that intersectionality within the outdoor community is most definitely present and must be addressed.

* * *

My previous definition of diversity in the outdoors has continually expanded as I followed this conversation over the past year. To be honest, I found this chapter the most difficult to write because the more I learned more about intersectionality and how that impacts a person's outdoor experience, the more I realized I didn't know. This past September, I was scrolling through my newsfeed and came across a post that Facebook's algorithm serendipitously suggested I might like (they know me so well). The post was published by The North Face, and depicted several photos of Tyrhee Moore, an accomplished mountaineer and outdoor education advocate. The post was accompanied by a snippet of Tyrhee's story: "Growing up my experience in the outdoors included mostly kids who looked like me. When I was sixteen years old, I traveled to Alaska for a backpacking course in the Talkeetna Range. On that course, I was one of two black kids out of the entire group. It wasn't until that moment that I realized there was and remains a tremendous adventure gap. More people of color should

11 Google Search, Google, www.google.com/search?ei=W2_mWvKSCsSxggfl84_
    YCA&q=definition%2Bof%2Bintersectionality&oq=definition%2Bof%2Bintersectionality&gs_
    l=psy-ab.3..0i67k1j0l5j0i22i10i30k1j0i22i30
    k1l3.4481.4481.0.5056.1.1.0.0.0.0.67.67.1.1.0....0...1.1.64.psy-ab..0.1.67....0.HG2gBP1NP40.

experience what it feels like to come alive in the outdoors. The future depends on it."

After scrolling through the accompanying photos, I excitedly set off to learn more about him and his outdoor adventures. Upon reading more about Tyrhee, I learned that he was born and raised right here in Washington, DC, and was a key player in the first all African-American climb of Denali. Enthusiastic about his story, I followed him on Instagram to learn more about how inspiring and influential men and women like him are promoting diversity in the Outdoors and to keep up with his upcoming adventures.

Several months later, Tyrhee posted a striking photo of a mountain range on Instagram celebrating the launch of a new coalition titled "Diversify Outdoors." His caption read: "As a proud member of this coalition, I am working alongside passionate outdoors men and women—bloggers, athletes, activists, and entrepreneurs—to promote diversity in outdoor spaces where people of color, LGBTQIA, and other diverse identities have historically been underrepresented. We are committed to promoting equity and access to the outdoors for all, that includes being body positive and celebrating people of all skill levels and abilities."

Many of these coalition leaders have not only accomplished incredible feats in the outdoors, they have dedicated their lives to improving the position of marginalized groups in the Outdoor Industry. One such leader, Diane Williams, founded Melanin Base Camp, an organization that has grown from an Instagram page to a website with eight adventure athlete bloggers.

Ambreen Tariq similarly founded her organization through Instagram. Tariq is the founder of @BrownPeopleCamping, a social media initiative that "utilizes personal narratives and digital storytelling to promote greater diversity in our public lands and outdoors community. Ambreen utilizes storytelling to share how her life experiences as a Muslim, South-Asian American immigrant female have shaped her love for the outdoors; to reflect more openly on the role privilege plays in enabling us to enjoy the outdoors; and to promote more passionately for everyone to experience and enjoy the outdoors in their own authentic ways".[12] Another prominent leader, Adriana Garcia, founded Latinx Hikers, "an online platform where Luz [Adriana's cofounder] and Adriana use their personal stories and photos to inspire, bring awareness and promote a culture of diversity and inclusiveness in the outdoors."[13] There are currently twenty-five leaders in the coalition that have founded impactful organizations. Collectively, their voices reach more than 154,000 followers on Instagram alone.

12   "Ambreen Tariq." Diversify Outdoors, www.diversifyoutdoors.com/tariq.

13   "Adriana Garcia." Diversify Outdoors, www.diversifyoutdoors.com/garcia.

* * *

America is changing, and for the better: "By 2042 whites will no longer comprise the majority of the population, according to the US Census Bureau, and research shows millennials are generally more tolerant and accepting than their parents about issues that involve minority groups, indicating a shift in the general social conscious, too. Even interracial marriages are at record levels. In short, our once majority white nation is morphing into a mosaic of colors."[14]

I believe increasing diversity in the outdoors requires a multifaceted and adaptable strategy. First and foremost, we must make a conscious effort to break down the barriers that discourage non-white participation in the outdoors. Barriers that are commonly cited include the high cost of gear and recreation activities, the fear of being hurt by others in the outdoors, a lack of companionship in outdoor activity, and a lack of self-belief.

I hope that in our lifetime, we will begin to see these barriers disseminate as general awareness of these barriers increases. I believe that even small-scale gear donations and individual contributions will make a palpable difference. As the sharing

14   Walker, Emma. "Diversity in the Outdoors: Why Does the Outdoor Industry (Still) Have a Diversity Problem?" RootsRated Media, 11 July 2017, rootsrated.media/blog/ the-outdoor-industry-still-has-a-diversity-problem/.

economy continues to grow, it's possible for us to implement various forms of peer-to-peer lending in an effort to further chip away at this barrier.

We must focus on the factors that motivate non-white participation in the outdoors and make those aspects of outdoor experience the focal point of outdoor media and culture. For example, the Outdoor Foundation survey found that "African Americans and Asian/Pacific Islanders, specifically, were motivated by the idea of enjoying nature with friends and family (58 and 57 percent, respectively, compared to Caucasians' 40 percent)."[15] Outdoor groups and media sources have the ability to emphasize this communal aspect of the outdoors in their communications, and that emphasis could go a long way in encouraging a sense of welcomeness and genuine belonging. Communicating a sense of belonging will require intentional, authentic, and personalized interactions.

* * *

After several weeks of thought, I have formed a more thorough response to Professor Park's important question: "Which women are you talking about?"

---

15   Walker, Emma. "Diversity in the Outdoors: Why Does the Outdoor Industry (Still) Have a Diversity Problem?" RootsRated Media, 11 July 2017, rootsrated.media/blog/the-outdoor-industry-still-has-a-diversity-problem/.

I am only writing about the women I have spoken to and writing about the trends that have presented themselves in their experiences and in my own experience. I recognize that my experience and that of the women I interviewed only narrowly covers the wide variety of experiences of the "female outdoor athlete."

I cannot speak for every woman I interviewed, but I grew up with abundant access to the outdoors. I am grateful for that and am now very aware that these privileges have biased my assessment of the modern female experience in the outdoors. I will graduate from college and in doing so, will enter into the Outdoor Industry with an advantage that many women will never have. I have had the opportunity to intimately study the Outdoor Industry this semester and will use this knowledge in my career.

As I move forward and attempt to discuss the impact of gender in the Outdoor Industry, I remain conscious that access to the outdoors means different things for different women. I simply hope that this conversation can be used as a starting place—a platform to eventually address other and more complex factors at play.

3

YOU KNOW WHAT THEY SAY ABOUT ASSUMING

———

April 2007, age 10. Gymnasium, Mendon Center Elementary School, Rochester, NY.

Beeeep.

The bell rang signaling the end of the fifth period. I closed my books excitedly and fell into line with the rest of my fifth-grade class. We waited for our teacher to close down the projector, abuzz with excitement to be heading to gym class. It was finally getting warm enough to go outside, and Mr. Smith, our gym teacher, had promised a game of kickball last Tuesday. Our teacher led us to the changing rooms, allowing us to stop at our lockers on the way to pick up our gym clothes.

Feeling fresh in my Avril Lavigne t-shirt, I walked into the gym with a few of my girlfriends, giggling about the fact that our teacher had just made two boys play both Romeo and Juliet in our English period. Just as we were about to fall into place jogging around the room with the rest of our classmates, I overheard Mr. Smith telling a classmate of mine that boys were better at sports than girls, period. In that moment, my not-so-little fifth-grade self was filled with rage. Coming from a family of athletic and empowered women, I couldn't believe what I was hearing.

At 5'10," I was a tall and athletic girl in elementary school. I towered over Mr. Smith, and I wasn't his biggest fan. Being the outspoken and somewhat ignorant fifth grader I was, I left the circle of my girlfriends and marched over to him, saying, "Mr. Smith, do you really think boys are better than girls at sports, period?"

I so distinctly remember his soft chuckle as he looked up at me and said, "Yes, Maryn. They are."

I found his response quite alarming. "I don't think that's true! I really don't…" I began to say.

"It's true. You should accept it," he interrupted.

"Oh yeah?" I sassed. "I will arm wrestle any boy in this room."

Looking back now, I am proud of my bravery.

He laughed with a twinkle in his eye and said, "Any boy?"

"Any boy," I said taking a defiant stance. He had his pick of the class as he watched my classmates circle around us, running their warm-up laps. I watched, unwavering, eying the small boys that skipped passed us.

"Hmm…" he amusedly pretended to ponder. "Hey, Colton! Come over here!"

As the biggest kid in our class stomped over to us, I felt my eyes widen.

"You said any boy…" he said, looking up at me with a grin.

Colton and I arm wrestled right there on the gym floor. I lost, to no one's surprise. I didn't say anything after our arm wrestle. I just stood up, brushed off my gym shorts, and jogged into place with the rest of the class. Our subsequent kickball game felt like the longest gym period of my life.

I felt upset for the rest of the day, thinking that maybe Mr. Smith was right. Maybe boys were just better than girls, period. It wasn't until I returned home and my mom put things back into perspective that I regained my confidence. She explained how inappropriate Mr. Smith's behavior was and told me I was so much more capable than people like Mr. Smith would ever realize. She pointed out that I didn't need those people to realize and recognize my capabilities. I just had to believe that I am strong and I am capable. Thanks, Mom.

* * *

We know that being outside is important for women, as it benefits their mental and physical health, but before I began to research the Outdoor Industry, I had a very narrow perception of what it meant to work and play outdoors. I knew little about what women were actually experiencing outside, what barriers prevented them from getting outside, and what factors prevented them from enjoying their time outside.

The Outdoor Industry is defined by the Outdoor Industry Association as including a broad range of activities, including snow sports, water sports, camping, fishing, off-roading, and hunting. Given this vast array of ways to participate in the outdoors, there are hundreds of different ways to make money in the Outdoor Industry. From outdoor education instructing, trip guiding, and environmental conservation work to coaching and being a sponsored athlete, there are many paths to choose. For the purposes of this book, I've defined working in the Outdoor Industry as somehow making a living through one of these activities—through sponsorship, coaching, or another form of paid adventuring. There are also hundreds of unique corporate paths within the Outdoor Industry that sound equally as inspiring. I have also explored the experience of women who have pursued a more traditional career path and have succeeded in balancing other work with their passion in the outdoors.

* * *

I couldn't help but return to that outdated, stale-smelling gymnasium when I began to research what it would be like to work in the Outdoor Industry. Mr. Smith introduced me to the wrongful assumption that lies frequently unnoticed at the foundation of the Outdoor Industry. That assumption is that men are superior to women, period. Exactly ten years later, I have formulated a response to Mr. Smith and all those who hold strong to the outdated and inaccurate assumption that men are superior to women in the outdoors—gender plays a smaller role in a person's outdoor athletic performance than they think it does.

This chapter showcases four women who are actively involved and kicking butt in the Outdoor Industry. These women have described moments where they have faced gender bias in their industry as a result of this assumption that men are superior to women. I enjoyed talking to these women because their stories showed that although there is a bias that impacts women in the industry, these challenges can be overcome. These women kick ass and someday I will, we will, too.

* * *

I have learned that there is significant variance between the perceived and the actual difference between male and female ability. In other words, the actual gap between female and male ability is much smaller than society commonly makes it out to be. This discovery was discouraging because it accentuated the fact that women are not given the credit they deserve. This discovery was exciting because it showed me that women are more capable than I have been led to believe.

I am not arguing that women can do everything that men can do—after all, we are built differently. Men naturally have more muscle and therefore men naturally have more brute strength. I am arguing that despite the male strength advantage, women are frequently capable of competing with men in many outdoor activities, and society does not recognize this potential for women to do so. I also wish to point out that in the sports where women are unable to compete directly with men due to their strength disadvantage, women still deserve more credit than the credit they are currently given.

The stories I gathered in my interviews paint a vivid picture of our society's opinion of the female outdoor athlete. Although

I went into my interviews knowing that women are the under-dogs in the Outdoor Industry, I was continually surprised by the extent to which even the most talented and badass women are looked down upon in their outdoor activities.

* * *

One of the first articles I came across was titled: "What Does It Mean to Be a Woman in the Outdoor Industry?" by Kim Kircher.[16] As my eyes scanned the first paragraph, I became excited about what I had found. I leaned in, made the window full screen and began to read again, more slowly, from the top.

Kim is currently working at Crystal Mountain, a ski resort in Washington State. She is one of the four female ski patrol directors in the United States. In her article, she discusses the challenges of working as a female patroller in a male-dom-inated industry, and how she has learned after years in the industry that she need not sacrifice her femininity in order to do her job well. I knew I had to reach out to her.

As I dialed Kim's number that next Tuesday, my heart was beating a little faster than usual. I had sat watching the clock for the past seven minutes, waiting for the clock to strike 6 p.m. my time, or 3 p.m. her time, and had Googled the Eastern

16   "What Does It Mean to Be a Woman in the Outdoor Industry?" Kim Kircher, 29 May 2015,
      kimkircher.com/2015/05/29/what-does-it-mean-to-be-a-women-in-the-outdoor-industry/.

Time Zone to Pacific Time Zone conversion, just to make sure that I had done my math right.

After watching the clock click to 6 p.m., I took a deep breath and dialed the number she had listed in her email. After two short rings, I heard a pleasant, "Hello?"

After brief introductions and a few minutes of chatting about the weather and Kim's article, I began my questions. I had several general questions on my pad in front of me, but after getting through the first few about her background in the industry and her current job, I decided to ditch my questions.

"Do you feel your gender has impacted your experiences in the outdoors?" I asked.

"That's a big question," she laughed. "Of course my gender has impacted my experiences in a big way."

"Can you think of any particular experiences where you keenly felt the effects of your gender?"

"Yeah, too many to count," she continued. "The first moment that comes to mind was on a patrol shift a few years ago. It was an icy day on the mountain, and one of my fellow patrollers, Brent, had just responded to an accident in a steep area. He called over the radio and asked for assistance because he was in a funky spot where the conditions were unsafe. He needed a toboggan and belay pack and I was the first to respond to him. When I arrived, the injured person looked at me, and then he looked back to Brent. He once again looked up at me, and then back to Brent, asking "Can't you get a dude?'"

Brent replied with confidence, saying, "You know, between Kim and me, we have fifty years of patrol experience. If I was injured, I would want Kim to come after me…You're gonna be fine, buddy."

The injured person finally agreed to be helped, and Kim said that although she felt fine about helping him, she still "laid it on thick with him, in terms of showing him how confident she was."

Kim went on to say that the most interesting part of this exchange was that when they made it down to the base, and the man was feeling better and was no longer afraid, he started to flirt with her. All this man could see her as was either "weak or somebody to be hit on." He couldn't just see her as a potential rescuer.

* * *

A female in the outdoors is seen as a woman before she is seen as an athlete or a rescuer, and assumptions are made quickly. Something else that struck me about this story is just how upfront and blatant this man was in his prejudice. He didn't stutter or struggle to articulate his concern about Kim's abilities in a politically correct way. He didn't have a problem wearing his sexist attitude on his sleeve. Perhaps this is because he didn't see sexism in the outdoors as incorrect, politically or otherwise.

Kim's experience shows that bias exists in the Outdoor Industry, and this industry can be an unattractive workplace for this reason. But Kim also shared stories that illustrate the genuine and unique rewards of her work. She spends her days outside, doing what she loves and has no regrets in choosing this path.

* * *

Almost every other woman I interviewed has confronted similar biased assumptions in her respective field. Zoe Balaconis, an avid adventurer and the senior editor of *Misadventures* magazine, told me "It's a regular occurrence when I'm surfing that men will assume I shouldn't be where I am, that I'm a danger to myself and others, or that I'm looking for advice."

Kitty Calhoun, one of the most accomplished professional alpine climbers in the sport, shared a similar experience. She said, "One time I was guiding on Denali and volunteered to go down early on summit day with a client who wasn't feeling well. Some young guy saw me returning to high camp and said, 'Don't worry. There is always another day.' He did not realize that I was a guide, and didn't know that I had already summited peaks higher and harder than the W. Buttress of Denali."

Sally McCoy, a talented outdoor athlete and the previous CEO of CamelBak, summited Mount Everest in 1987. As she said in a keynote speech a few years ago, she went for weeks without outside contact during that climb and weathered one of the fiercest blizzards to hit Everest to date. Sally said that if her climb ever comes up in casual conversation with a man, the man frequently starts lecturing her on how to climb Everest. She says she listens for a while, and then she asks him, "When were you on Everest?" and more often than not, he responds, "Oh, I saw it in Imax."

Adriene Levknecht, one of the most skilled professional kayakers in the world, shared that a few years ago, she and her boyfriend, Snowy, traveled to the Green River in North Carolina to go for a kayak. Adriene and Snowy were meeting up with Snowy's friend, who was also a kayaker. When they stepped out of the car, Snowy's friend looked at Adriene, looked back at Snowy and said, "Oh, nice, is your lady gonna run shuttle for us?"

The person who "runs shuttle" doesn't kayak, but instead transports the kayakers up and down the river between their trips. Adriene is the seven-time Green Race Champion and record holder, and she is more than comfortable tackling the difficult rapids on the Green River. Snowy responded, "No. Actually, she'll probably run more rapids than you." And sure enough, she did.

These snippets, and so many more that I have not the space to include, show that people in our society are biased by an athlete's gender. Even the most accomplished and skilled female outdoor athletes are judged—by amateurs and experts alike—simply because they are female.

It is impossible for me to imagine an injured skier questioning a male ski patrol director or an inexperienced male lecturing an experienced male climber about what it's like to climb Everest. It is almost harder for me to imagine a kayaking athlete immediately assuming that a man climbing out of a car with kayaking gear is only there to cheer on and assist the other men. Facing such assumptions is uniquely part of the female experience.

* * *

All of these offenses appear to be small on the surface. A quick comment here, an ignorant question there—these moments could be labeled as insignificant. Many men and women do label them as insignificant.

These small instances add up and create an unwelcoming and uncomfortable atmosphere for women in the outdoors. This disrespect has become normalized. The women in the Outdoor Industry often don't have any choice but to "shake it off" and move on to the more important tasks at hand. Kim had to brush off the offensive comment from the injured man and carry on doing her job. Zoe didn't have time to stop and address the demeaning nature of her fellow surfer's commentary. She had to paddle out to catch the next wave.

When Kitty descended Denali early that day, and the guy at the bottom said, "Don't worry. There's always another day." Kitty responded simply by saying, "Yeah, I hope so," and walked away. When I heard this my heart leaped a little, and I felt proud. I thought, "Hell yeah, she's right. No need to waste energy on such a ridiculous interaction. She is way above that ignorant bystander, and she can prove it." Many other elite female athletes I heard from had a similar response when they were disrespected. They don't grant this ignorance attention. They let their performance do the talking. I was left inspired by their confidence, courage, and grit.

As I spoke to my friends about these cool stories, we enjoyed picturing these strong women kicking the butts of the men who doubted them. After discussing Adriene's story, my friend Jacky brought up an interesting point, saying, "I love that Adriene just pushed her kayak in the water and left those guys in her wake. I would've loved to watch that! She has to have some genuine courage and confidence in her ability to let her performance do the talking. I wish I was that good at something."

After my other friends echoed similar sentiments, I realized that not all women in the outdoors feel that they can allow their performance to do the talking when they are confronted by bias. For example, although I love to rock climb, I know I have little experience and skill in the sport. If I were descending from a mountain early, as Kitty did when she was a guide, I would have been deeply impacted by the onlooker's comments. I likely would have been discouraged and ashamed by my lack of skill and would have felt less inclined to return to Denali.

I don't mean to speak for any of these elite athletes and claim that they were not affected by those who treated them disrespectfully. There is no doubt in my mind that this bias affects all women, no matter their skill level. I just feel it's important to point out that the effects of that bias and the woman's response to that bias may be different depending on a woman's skill and confidence level.

Overall, if gender bias is this prevalent and impactful among the most accomplished and established women in Outdoor Sport, it is without a doubt impacting all women who participate in the outdoors—no matter their chosen activity or intensity level.

* * *

I recognize that females face these biases and assumptions in almost every modern facet of society, but it appears that gender bias in the outdoors isn't questioned, studied or challenged as frequently as it is in other areas. This gender bias needs to be studied, questioned, and *prioritized as a serious issue* in our modern society.

Despite the challenges, the women interviewed for this book have shown us that we can succeed. There are women out there, doing it, and they don't want to be doing anything else. They are living out their passion. The girls of our generation are the lucky ones because we can stand on their shoulders.

PART 2

FACTORS AT PLAY

I will not let anyone walk through my mind with their dirty feet.

—MAHATMA GANDHI

4

HOW EQUAL ARE WE?

———

August 2015, Age 19. Junior Sailing Center, The Rochester Yacht Club, Rochester, NY.

It was a windy and stormy day on Lake Ontario, with the gusts reaching a velocity of up to thirty knots. I sat in the back of a shallow Boston Whaler, twisting the tiller handle forward and back to rev up and slow the engine. I was more or less attempting to hold my position in the waves (while selfishly minimizing the spray that came over the bow) as my group of sailors circled around me, gathering up for our sail into the docks. Although it was only 11:30 a.m., the sky was dark, and given that the wind was coming from the north, the waves were climbing up to heights of five feet.

"Nice work, John! Remember to pull in that sail!" I yelled over the sound of the wind as John joined our circle and fell into place between two more confident sailors. I was so proud of him for being out in this breeze today. I had coached him last summer, when he was afraid to push off the dock.

I blew one long whistle and strategically steered my whaler through a gap in their circling boats, heading toward the pier. Their boats fell into line behind me. In some ways, we were lucky the wind was coming from the north because it meant that as we sailed south toward the docks, we could remain more organized going downwind. Nonetheless, the waves complicated this downwind leg, and before we had reached the piers, we had two more capsizes. I circled back to help the boys right and bail out their swamped boats, the rest of my sailors swerving into safety position like a well-oiled machine.

It was only Monday, but I felt exhausted by the time we hit the docks and I tied my coach boat up after our morning session. I coached the youth race team, which meant I had spent most of the summer hanging out with twelve fun and troublesome boys between the ages of ten to fourteen. They were a rowdy bunch, and their skills varied widely.

After a hefty PB&J and few competitive games of Foursquare, our lunch break was over. It was my fourth summer coaching at the Yacht Club, and although I felt comfortable handling these conditions, I asked my boss if one of my coworkers could assist me with the afternoon session. The breeze was building and I knew my guys could handle it, but I thought it would be safer to have another coach on the water. It certainly would be nice to have another set of hands to bail.

My boss agreed, and transferred another employee, Stephen, over to help me in the afternoon. I thanked Stephen for his help, zipped up my spray jacket, and hopped into the whaler. As we were pushing off the dock, my boss said, "Alright, Stephen, take good care of 'em out there," and he gave Stephen the walkie-talkie. I didn't think much of his parting comments. I just revved our motor and waved goodbye.

* * *

Women have much to benefit from being in the outdoors but face unique barriers that make this time in the outdoors less pleasurable, and in some cases, prevents them from participating in outdoor sport to begin with. The first barrier that surfaced in my research stems from the assumption that men are superior to women. This assumption leads to verbal and nonverbal discrimination in the outdoors. This discrimination takes the form of a small comment here, and a questioning look there. I decided to dig deeper into the occurrence of this discrimination. Is it possible that this discrimination only exists in instances where a woman's physical qualities truly do put her at a disadvantage? In other words, could a person attempt to justify this discrimination, saying it is limited to occasions where the female body is indeed, for scientific reasons, less physically able than the man's body?

In considering the *actual* difference between male and female ability in the Outdoor Industry, I thought back on this moment. Any objective bystander looking into the boat would have seen two sailing coaches. Removing gender from the equation, one coach was twenty years old, had three full summers of coaching experience, and had been working with these sailors for the past three weeks. The other was eighteen years old, had three weeks of coaching experience, and had never worked with these sailors before. One coach was female, and one coach was male.

As the more experienced coach in this situation, I brought several assets to the team that Stephen did not. I was more qualified to deal with the situations that were bound to present themselves that afternoon. I had more knowledge of the skillsets of each individual sailor and a stronger relationship with the group as a whole; and yet, my boss told Stephen to "take care of 'us'" and handed him the walkie-talkie. Just for context, I was five inches taller than Stephen, and I was likely stronger than him. (I will never know for sure, but I can tell you it would've been a close fight!) The only reason Stephen was treated as more capable and qualified in this situation was that Stephen was a boy, and I was a girl.

In that little boat three years ago, my boss assumed that I had a disadvantage in my job, but I knew I actually had mental and physical advantages my male peer did not. This is the incorrect assumption that so often leads to discrimination. Is this a trend? I decided to take a closer look at the stories I had gathered from the women I had spoken to. Many echoed the same experience I had. The common thread seemed to be the assumption that men are physically and mentally superior to women in outdoor athletics, even when they objectively are not.

* * *

In general, women have fewer muscles than men and an aerobic disadvantage due to lower testosterone levels. However, women have a greater range of motion due to their more flexible joints and their bodies are more efficient at converting glycogen to energy. This increased efficiency in energy conversion leads women to have an overall endurance advantage. This endurance advantage surfaces in extreme endurance sports because females' bodies burn energy more efficiently over the long haul. This allows them to build up a stronger level of endurance as intensity increases. Women are able to compete with men in extreme endurance sports, such as ultramarathon running, long distance swimming, and long distance thru-hiking.[17]

When I read about this trend, I was pretty excited. The female body is far more capable than I have given it credit for. It has abilities that the male body does not. Even if I don't end up working in or participating in the endurance sector of the Outdoor Industry, it builds my confidence to know that science shows women can hold their own in some of the most challenging outdoor activities. I decided to study this trend in the real world. Are women competing with men in extreme endurance sports? Are women given the credit they deserve for their superior endurance skills?

* * *

Jennifer Pharr Davis is an American long distance hiker. In 2011, she set the speed record for hiking the Appalachian Trail in just forty-six days, beating the previous endurance record by twenty-six hours. On that day, she was the fastest hiker to walk that trail—man or woman. Jennifer's hike showcased that a woman can indeed surpass the endurance mark of a man.

Three years later, Scott Jurek, the most decorated ultrarunner in the United States, set out to break her record. As a champion ultrarunner, Jurek regularly competes in ultramarathons,

---

17   Crowther, Greg. "Gender and Endurance Performance." Gender and Endurance Performance, faculty.washington.edu/crowther/Misc/RBC/gender.shtml.

races that surpass fifty kilometers in distance. Before Jurek even stepped foot on the trail, he had proven his impressive endurance capabilities.

Jurek succeeded in beating Jennifer's record, but only by three hours. Jennifer was surprised by the small margin of his victory—a mere 0.3 percent. She approached him to ask how she could compete so closely with him as a woman who had never won an ultrarace.

Jurek was not surprised by his narrow victory, and responded, "The gender gap diminishes and disappears over distance… When you're traveling over two thousand miles, it doesn't matter if you are male or female. Superhuman powers are superhuman powers; they know no gender, no age."[18] Jurek's attitude is respectful, and directly supports scientific fact. I'm a fan.

* * *

Ginger Bruns, an impressive endurance athlete and outdoor education guide at Georgetown University, also believes women are on equal footing with men in most endurance activities. During our interview, she said, "At the heart of

---

18 Press, The Associated. "Appalachian Record Set." The New York Times, The New York Times, 13 July 2015, www.nytimes.com/2015/07/14/sports/appalachian-record-set. html?mtrref=www.google.com&gwh=8497BD86C33567FF99B8E12619E603C3&gwt=pay.

endurance sports, there's no time to question if you can do it or not because you're a woman. You just do it. It's a mental thing."

I was inspired by Jennifer's accomplishments, Jurek's comments, and Ginger's attitude. They have shown that women have earned the right to be treated as equals in the endurance sports community. I decided to reach out to another endurance athlete, Kate Worteck, to see her point of view on this matter.

Kate Worteck is an ultramarathon runner and an avid long-distance backpacker from the San Francisco Bay area. I had read an article Kate wrote for *Elle* about female gear options and was captivated by her comments and experiences.

Kate pointed out a regular occurrence on the hiking trail. "When other hikers asked me for directions, they'll address the man in our group, even when I'm the person holding the map." Kate said it's not only on the trail that men are considered superior. Her boyfriend is an ultra-marathoner, and when new friends hear about his latest trail race, there is immediate awe and admiration; however, when she mentions her latest solo backpacking trip, the response is not one of awe and admiration, it is one of concern. They ask: "Weren't you scared? Isn't that dangerous?"

From her time in the endurance community, Kate has realized

that even her closest friends see a female hiker as a "slow-moving target in Tevas," rather than a strong and experienced athlete. It is scientifically proven that women have assets men do not on the trails, and yet they are still treated as inferior.

* * *

Another interesting area to study is the sport of climbing. There is no specialized gender equipment, and the difficulty rating of a climb does not change according to gender. Most importantly, both men and women have climbed at the most elite level of 5.15. Despite the myth that the male's build allows for climbing superiority, the female's flexibility and statistically smaller size give her certain advantages that often allow her to climb at the same level.

Many climbers assert that "It's not what you have. It's how you use it," and they emphasize that the majority of variance between climbers' abilities can be attributed to training and technique. Their perception is supported by the fact that women are often able to compete directly with men. Given the fact that climbing allows the female's physical qualities to shine, do women in the climbing community feel as if they are treated as equals with men? Does our modern climbing community portray the sport as an equal playing field for both genders?

Last September, the woman's climbing community *Flash Foxy* released a survey asking climbers how gender affects their experience in the climbing gym. The group was interested in collecting data about microaggressions, behavior that includes "unwanted staring and advice, physical and verbal harassment... and general discomfort in specific areas of the gym." The survey received over 1,500 responses and 70 percent of those responses from females. The data collected indicates that females often are considered inferior climbers and are treated as such.

65 percent of female respondents said they had experienced microaggressions while climbing, while only 25 percent of men responded in the same way. This means that over two times more women than men feel as if their time at the gym has been marked by degrading assumptions, unwelcome commentary, and condescending advice.

Additionally, 39 percent of women said they had experienced unwanted staring. This was more than double the number of men that reported the same experience. It is important to note that the overwhelming majority of women stated that these microaggressions came from men. The survey found that sometimes female climbers are treated so poorly that their experience at the climbing gym is not enjoyable. This should not be the case, especially given the facts that show women successfully compete with men in the sport.

Katharine R. Plate, a skilled climber and author of the article "Rock Climbing is a Masculine Sport? Understanding the complex gendered subculture of rock climbing," wrote the following after a climb one night at the mountain:

"*I notice the pain in my throat from the deep thirst I have acquired throughout the day, and I take a deep gulp from my water bottle. As I set it back down to continue basking in this wonderful feeling of bliss, I sense a presence in front of me. It is an older man, one I have seen around, but have never met. He gives me a quizzical look, and then looks over at the climb I just led, where my friends are currently top roping. He looks back at me and asks, 'Did you lead that?'*

'Yeah,' I reply, curious about his question. He looks back over at my group of friends, two men and two women, and then back at me. 'So…are you the strongest climber in your group?' he asks. I think for a second, realizing that I am, but still wondering why he cares to point it out. 'I guess I am, at least here at the Creek,' I say. He continues to have that somewhat confused look on his face, grunts. 'Huh,' he tells me, 'I'm impressed,' and walks away. I sit there for a while longer trying to decipher the cryptic conversation I just had but I look at the sunset again and feel a growl in my stomach, it's time to head back to camp for dinner.

The conversation I had with that man didn't register until later that night when I realized that he wasn't just surprised because

I, a woman, could lead a difficult climb. It was the fact that I was the most competent climber in a group of both men and women. I couldn't figure out what was so perplexing about the situation until I realized that he is probably more accustomed to climbing as a male-dominated sport than I am. Surely, he knows of strong female climbers, but he might not be used to women being stronger and leading their male partners."[19]

* * *

As I reflected on these stories, I felt confused. In two sports where females are at least equal with men, (and arguably have the upper hand—many females have proven this to be the case!) females are treated as if they are the underdogs. Given these trends, it is not surprising that I have lived my whole life believing that females are at a disadvantage in the Outdoor Industry.

I decided to continue to reach out to athletes, in hopes that I would find some congruency between a female's actual ability in her sport and society's view of her ability in her sport. A few days after speaking to Kate, I reached out to Moona Whyte. Moona is a talented professional kitesurfer, who competes on the professional circuit.

---

19   Plate, Katharine R. "Rock Climbing Is a Masculine Sport? Understanding the Complex Gendered Subculture of Rock Climbing. ." www.sheffield.ac.uk/polopoly_fs/1.71699!/file/10-Plate-article.pdf.

When I asked Moona about the role gender plays in the physical act of kitesurfing, she answered that because men are stronger, they can often ride at a different level than women. However, she went on to say that "[w]ith kitesurfing, being super strong is not a necessity. You're not paddling and creating your own speed like in surfing; the kite pulls you into a wave and through your turns, so it is almost more about technique than strength." She explained that gender doesn't play a large role in wave riding, and *if women believe in themselves*, they can "hit the lip or pull into a barrel, just like the guys."

Moona's testament shows that although there is a slight gender-related gap in kitesurfing, the gap is not as large as we have made it out to be. She pointed out that the small gap in physical ability certainly cannot explain or account for the significantly fewer sponsorship opportunities for women in kitesurfing, and the drastically less interest in female kitesurfing athletes overall. This sponsorship injustice is not unique to the sport of kitesurfing, as women's sport sponsorship only accounted for 0.4 percent of total sports sponsorship between 2011 and 2013.[20]

Nina Burakowski, a freelance writer and outdoor enthusiast, echoed Moona's thoughts regarding female kiteboarding after ten years of honing her kiteboarding skills. She admitted

---

20 "Sponsorship & Media." Women In Sport, www.womeninsport.org/how-were-doing-it/sponsorship-media/.

to being concerned that she lacked the strength required to participate before she took that first lesson so long ago. She quickly learned that the sport is more about finesse and grace than brute strength, and pointed out that even in strong winds, she can maneuver her kite with one or two fingers. In her experience, the only gender barrier in the sport is mental and is wholly rooted in societal perceptions. The International Kiteboarding Association estimates that only 10 percent of kiteboarders are female. Nina speculates that females are less likely to believe they can succeed in an "extreme sport," and this doubt is the big barrier to participation. She calls for us to break down this barrier, and says that "learning to kiteboard will initially put anyone out of their comfort zone but like other outdoor pursuits, the power of the sport comes from teaching us self-reliance and resilience. I come back from every session on the water feeling stronger about myself and knowing that I've challenged myself into doing something that not everyone has the tenacity to do."[21]

* * *

Moona's and Nina's comments about the potential mental and emotional barriers to outdoor participation stuck with me. Moona said that "…if women believe in themselves, they can hit the lip or pull into a barrel, just like the guys." This

21 Burakowski, Nina. "Why Kiteboarding Is for Girls." Misadventures Magazine, misadventuresmag.com/why-kiteboarding-is-for-girls/.

comment helped me realize that my research did not touch upon society's perceived *mental* differences between men and women in the outdoors. Several interviewees shared with me that researchers have found that although women tend to be more risk-averse in adventure sports, women often use better judgment in the wilderness. Females are less likely to overestimate their abilities and therefore make more reflective decisions in dangerous scenarios.

I had not considered women as incapable in a wilderness setting, but I certainly had not seen them as superior to men in this way. I wanted to see if this seldom-talked-about female asset was recognized in the Outdoor Industry.

I called Cori Coccia, a skilled solo-hiker and the current program director at *Girl Ventures*, a nonprofit based in San Francisco. She mentioned that she encounters varying reactions when she tells people about her solo-trips—ranging from people saying, "Oh rad, tell me more about that... I would love to do that myself!" to people feeling outright threatened by her. Some assume she has to carry a gun.

Cori has faced discrimination on the trails because she is a woman traveling alone. Other hikers often assume she is with a group and become uncomfortable when they realize she is not. Cori believes she often isn't seen as a capable traveler; she is seen as a vulnerable woman traveling alone in an environment she cannot handle. Her survival assets are not acknowledged. Cori pointed out that when you're a woman hiking alone, "people think you're crazy or there is something wrong with you; whereas if you're man, it's kinda like ooh, wild woodsman. [Men] get all this credit for being brave, or strong, but women get very stigmatized." Cori's experience illustrates a severe injustice that plays out in our modern Outdoor Industry. Female athletes' skills are downplayed, and their mental and physical advantages are ignored (and in many cases outright denied).

But I do not believe this should discourage women from pursuing a career in the Outdoor Industry. The bottom line is women have assets that men do not, and we should not allow our culture to ignore them. Not only do men lack awareness of women's capabilities, women often lack awareness of their own capabilities. This needs to change, and I am confident it will. The bias in the Outdoor Industry is not rooted in scientific fact, and we are stronger than society has led us to believe.

* * *

After my research, I can confidently say that the short answer is no, discrimination does not only exist in instances where a woman's physical qualities truly do put her at a disadvantage. In other words, there is no way a person can attempt to justify this discrimination, even by saying it is limited to occasions where the female body is indeed, for scientific reasons, less physically able than the man's body. This discrimination exists in every realm of outdoor activity, even in arenas where the female body has specific advantages that the male body does not have. Although this discovery was not surprising, it emphasizes the gross injustice inherent in this discrimination. In doing this research, I quickly learned how much we, as young women, have to learn about our own capabilities in the outdoors. Many women remain unaware of the advantages of being a female in the outdoors. We are so much more capable than we think.

Thinking back to that windy day a few summers ago, I realized that I should have stood up to my boss. I should have pointed out that it was not cool of him to tell Stephen to "take care of us." I, as a woman, should have realized the assets I had. I should have put more stock into my own ability.

5

MEDIA MADNESS

———

December 2015, Age 20. Home, Rochester, NY.

"Dude, check this out! This is what I was telling you about!" my twin sister said excitedly as I meandered into the kitchen, eyes still sleepy from my first good night's sleep in a long time. It was the first day of my Christmas vacation, and I was happy to be home. My twin, Terese, had gotten home from the University of Southern California a few days before me. When I walked into the kitchen, I found her sitting on our kitchen counter, engrossed in her phone. From the looks of the bowl of soggy Special K sitting beside her, it appeared she had been sitting this way for quite some time.

I slid over to her in my slippers and put my chin on her shoulder, peeping at her phone to see what all her fuss was about.

She tapped the screen and the Instagram video started over again. Sara Hughes, one of Terese's beach volleyball teammates, was doing a series of full-length pull-ups on two hanging ropes in the training gym. Her form was flawless, and her strength was impressive.

"Whoa...play it again," I said. Terese and I sat there for more than four minutes replaying the video, exchanging words of admiration and excitement.

Of course, I had seen people do pull-ups on a rope before. I spend a good deal of time in the training room. I also follow several fitness accounts on social media and had seen similar videos on Instagram and Facebook. No video had impacted me like this one, though. There was something powerful about seeing a girl my own age doing something I previously had thought myself incapable of.

For the remainder of that Christmas break, Terese and I went to the gym on days we might have previously written off as vacation days. We worked out with renewed motivation. I had decided I was going to master the pull-up. And then I was going to do some pull-ups on ropes.

With Sara's strength in my mind's eye, I stayed motivated for the next several months. I put in special effort to strengthen my bicep and latissimus muscles. "If Sara can do it, I can do it," I thought. I am proud to say that by the end of the spring I was able to bang out four pull-ups.

* * *

In the first quarter of 2016, US adults spent 10 hours and 39 minutes consuming media every day. While this number seemed extreme to me at first, the term "media" in this statistic covers a wide variety of publications and digital platforms, including social media sites such as Facebook and Instagram, and news sites such as CNN, HuffingtonPost, and Buzzfeed. When I stop to break down my daily media usage, I would say 10 hours sounds about right. We are surrounded by visual input all day, every day.

Given our modern infatuation with imagery and social media, it makes sense that these various forms of media have a huge impact on our reality—even when we do not consciously analyze what we are seeing. Media matters. Does our media inspire and encourage female participation in the outdoors? Or, does it pose as another barrier to female participation in the outdoors?

* * *

"If they can do it, I can do it." Leah Evans said on the phone, all the way from Rossland, British Columbia. Leah is a professional skier, and the founder of Canada's only all-girls Freeski camp provider, *Girls Do Ski*. Leah was in the midst of telling me about the moment she decided to forfeit her full ride to university to chase her passion: skiing. She said this decision was inspired by two girls her very age. She said she saw them from afar at a ski race and realized that they were living the life she yearned for. "If they can do it, I can do it," she said.

I hung up the phone that day feeling so inspired by Leah's courage, passion, and determination. Leah hadn't even interacted with those two girls, yet their example inspired her to completely alter her life's path. All Leah needed to see was that it could be done. As I thought about Leah's story, I realized that she was right. Sometimes all we need in order to move forward is to see is that our dreams can be achieved, or that our goals are attainable.

Both Leah's story and my own experience with Sara inspiring a six-month-long pull-up challenge support the fact that visual inspiration is important to the female athlete. "Studies have found that whether we're six or thirty-six, seeing reflections of ourselves on the product's packaging makes us more likely to buy it and buy into its ethos. Women gravitate to things that have a female image or spokesperson, while men do the same."[22] Given this fact, I decided to look into outdoor brand media to see how the images and video footage portray the female outdoor athlete. Does the media make it look like our dreams can be achieved? Does it inspire in the way it has the potential to?

* * *

In a capstone research paper written by Jenna Williams, an experiment was conducted that aimed to answer these questions. Jenna began by analyzing the Instagram posts of ten prominent outdoor brands. The brands chosen to be included in this content analysis were Marmot, Patagonia, Black Diamond, Mountain Hardwear, Arc'teryx, REI, The North Face, Prana, Title Nine, and Athleta. Prana is female-focused while Title Nine and Athleta offer clothing for women only.

She examined the latest thirty posts from each brand and accessed how often men and women were included in these images. She found that in the pictures posted by co-ed brands, "68.9 percent included men while only 40.4 percent included women (only including pictures with people, including images where men and women were shown in groups).

22   [i] Bastone, Kelly. "We Need More Images of Women in Outdoor Media." Outside Online, Outside Magazine, 11 Apr. 2017, www.outsideonline.com/2172896/why-we-need REI. "2017 National Study on Women and the Outdoors." LinkedIn SlideShare, REI, 30 Mar. 2017, www.slideshare.net/REI_/2017-national-study-on-women-and-the-outdoors.

-women-outdoor-packaging.

This statistic shows that media reinforces the perception of the outdoors as a male-dominated space, and outdoor recreation as a masculine activity. Zofia Reych, a talented climber and anthropologist, articulately reacted to this trend in her article "The Problem of Female Athletes" saying: "Should this really come as a surprise? After all, the dominant discourse goes something like this: Girls are pretty, but they can't really do sports, so let's put a token girl in here and there. Make sure she looks really hot. After all, it's not about her skills, it's about her cute face. She will make men buy the magazine and make other women want to be like her, because men find her attractive. I mean, what other things could a woman possibly want from doing sports apart from finding a guy?"

Jenna went on to examine the intensity of each participant's activity. She found that "for women who are shown being active, 43 percent are shown engaged in an easy activity, 45 percent are shown engaged in a moderate activity, and 12 percent are shown engaged in an extreme activity. The inverse is true for men. For men who are shown being active, 19 percent are shown engaged in an easy activity, 33 percent are shown engaged in a moderate activity, and 48 percent are shown engaged in an extreme activity." It is also notable that Athleta and T9, the only all-female brands sampled, did not include any images that portrayed extreme activity.

Women are shown less than men in outdoor media and the

women that are shown in outdoor media are not shown in a variety of activity levels. These findings show that outdoor recreation advertisements featuring women are generally "more pleasant, less active, and more focused on playful activities..." instead of being more realistic and showing women participating in the challenging outdoor activities they do. Men are depicted in a variety of activities, and advertisements that showcase men typically illustrate an epic adventure or challenging feat.

This difference in representation undoubtedly contributes to gender bias in the Outdoor Industry. Outdoor media constricts the definition of the outdoorsy female and fails to show women as inspiring and positive *real* role models.

If you can see it, you can do it, and the media makes it so women don't see it.

The media focuses on the woman's body and sexuality, either blatantly or inadvertently. Jenna asserted that "sexualized and idealized images of female athletes seem to prompt a focus on one's own physical appearance, whereas performance images elicit a focus on one's own athleticism." It seems as if outdoor media does not inspire the way it has the potential to; but rather, it leads to insecurity and feelings of unworthiness. These images not only affect the world around us, they affect our opinions of ourselves.

* * *

In a report published by *Misadventures* magazine, titled "Gender Representation in Outdoor Industry Magazines," analysts study the low number of women represented in outdoor and adventure-industry publications. The *Misadventures* analysts closely studied the staff list, article bylines, photographs, and audience demographics in several popular magazines such as *Outside, Backpacker, Bicycling, Rock and Ice, Trail Runner*, and *Surfer*. What they found was pretty interesting, as in most cases male representation outnumbered female representation by a pretty staggering margin. Men outnumbered women in both the topics that were included within the magazine, and in the staff that wrote the magazine.

The chief offender of was *Surfer* magazine, where there are zero women on staff and ninety-eight men. There were, on average, thirteen men bylining articles and zero women. The observed issue included eighty-one images of men and only four images of women. These statistics were overwhelming to me, especially given that the description of *Surfer* under their "about" tab online reads: "Known as the 'bible of the sport,' SURFER Magazine has been the foremost authority on surf culture since its founding in 1960." If *Surfer* is indeed the "bible" and "the foremost authority" on surf culture, what does this mean for women in the sport?

Clearly, women do not have a say in creating surfing culture (seeing as there are no women on staff). This also means that in the eyes of this community, female surfers are not worthy of being included in their top end publications. Men are in control of the surfing culture and as shown by these figures, they feel little obligation to incorporate women. How many industries fail to question if it is okay to have a staff made entirely of men? Even *Men's Health* magazine has six women on their executive team of seventeen. This points back to the idea that gender bias in outdoor sports isn't questioned frequently or as vehemently as it is in other industries.

* * *

In Moona Whyte's interview, she claimed that although she "occasionally sees talented women doing cool tricks in kite-surfing media, most of the images [she sees] are a bit more feminine (all about the girl's style rather than power, hair blowing in the wind, wearing a bikini), and even just lifestyle shots (standing on the beach holding your gear in a bikini)."

One of Moona's sponsors actually encourages her to "do tutorials of simpler tricks while wearing a bikini, because if people see a girl doing something, it means they can probably do it too." Her experience shows that media makers purposefully limit talented women when portraying them to the general public.

Moona taught me that this biased portrayal of women in media not only impacts the audience, it also impacts the athlete. Moona showed that this biased treatment "demeans us, and makes us think [our sexuality is] all we are capable of, and all we should strive for. That sort of thing (like seeing brands or magazines value beauty or sexiness over talent and pushing the level of riding) almost makes me want to give up on charging harder…"

This bias in outdoor media needs to be talked about. Even more than that, it needs to be critically assessed so that a solution may bring it to an end. It clearly has broad reaching effects that harm many women directly, and even more women indirectly.

* * *

In the era of social media, influencer marketing has become a staple for many big outdoor brands. Due in part to these brands wanting to show off their fashionable gear and also in part to the trend of "Instagram fabrication," media portrayal of women in the outdoors has become somewhat fabricated. By "Instagram fabrication," I'm referring to the increasingly common practice of painstakingly staging a photo opportunity, so much so that the goal of the activity pictured is no longer to engage in the activity but to capture a cool picture. More commonly than not, when a woman is pictured in the outdoors, she is wearing trendy multicolored outdoor gear (that remains pristinely clean) and is staring out at picturesque terrain. She looks as if she effortlessly scaled that mountain—her hair remains perfectly curled and she shows no signs of sweat. These images dictate what the expectation is for women in the outdoors, and in doing so, disregard reality. As a result, increasing emphasis is placed on women's appearance in the backcountry, and trips have become more about creating an aesthetically pleasing image than taking on an adventure.

As Cassidy Randall, an accomplished freelance writer, stated in a recent article, "Of course any trend that inspires women to explore is a good thing, whether hiking one mile or fifteen, paddling a flat lake or big whitewater. But what message do these portrayals send to women about what outdoor adventures "should" be?"[23] The occurrence of this trend shows us that simply increasing female representation in outdoor media will not lead to the change that women deserve. As we make strides to increase female-focused outdoor media, we need to do so in a way that values the female for her athleticism and her uniqueness, not her ability to blend into a pretty picture or look attractive in the wilderness. In some ways, this will require intentionality, as our society is used to focusing on a woman's appearance. In other ways, this will require us to

23 Randall, Cassidy. "How Instagram Is Skewing the Way We Talk About Women in the Outdoors." Travel + Leisure, www.travelandleisure.com/trip-ideas/adventure-travel/women-adventurers.

abandon all intentionality, because women are accomplishing amazing feats in the outdoors, and all we need to do is capture those unedited moments.

Kristin Warkentin, an adventurer and *Misadventures* contributor, echoed this sentiment, saying: "The backcountry is literally the only place, aside from my living room couch, where I feel I have permission to stop thinking about my parrot nose, or whether my hair is getting wavy in only one direction again, or whether waxing my eyebrows will make the rest of my face look unkempt by comparison…It's not that I want to see fewer of the beautiful women who post their adventures on Instagram. If they are genuinely out there enjoying themselves, doing what they love in their own way, fantastic… As more and more women discover the benefits of getting outside, it might take some extra vigilance, some deliberateness, to ensure the hiking trail doesn't become another catwalk—just one more place for us to judge each other's appearances, and our own."[24]

* * *

Increased awareness of the shortcomings of outdoor media should inspire us to look at this media with a new lens. I am now aware of the fact that outdoor media does not accurately

24 "City Creep and the Perfect Outdoor Woman | Misadventures." Misadventures Magazine, 17 Dec. 2015, misadventuresmag.com/city-creep-and-the-perfect-outdoor-woman/.

showcase the power, strength, and general badass nature of women in the outdoors. These women are more inspiring in real life than they are in the magazine, and we need to bridge that gap.

I now think of Sara Hughes every time I walk past the muscle men sitting around the gym and jump up to the pull-up bars. Positive change can happen rapidly in outdoor media. There are a million Saras out there, and they just need to be seen, documented, and valued.

6

THE SKY DOESN'T FEEL LIKE OUR ONLY LIMIT

October 2016, Age 21. Prospect St, Georgetown University, Washington, DC.

It was an uncharacteristically warm night for October, and the sky had just begun to shift from a light pink to a deep purple hue. It had been raining all day, but the DC humidity was rapidly soaking up all the moisture that had pooled on the ground. I felt as if I was walking in a sauna as I jogged down the cobblestone sidewalk toward my friend Carrie's apartment. I was running late, as usual.

Out of breath, I knocked on her door and heard her bound down the stairs, saying, "It's open! Come on in, Mar!"

"Hi hi!" I squealed as I stepped through her door and we hugged. It had been a long week of midterms and I hadn't seen her for what felt like an eternity. We had been looking forward to tonight. We were headed to a twenty-first birthday party for one of my oldest friends, Brian, who Carrie had recently started dating. It was a long time coming and they made an adorable couple. I couldn't have been happier.

"I just have to grab my rain jacket!" she said as she ran back up the stairs, taking them two at a time.

"I don't think you need it!" I shouted after her. "It stopped… it feels like an August night out there!"

Five minutes later we were strolling down the sidewalk, arm in arm. Carefully avoiding the puddles from the recent rain, we chatted about this book. It was mid-semester, and I was filling her in on my topic and the cool women I had interviewed. A few blocks later, we ran into our friend Luke. He was also headed to Brian's and he fell into step beside us. After exchanging our happy greetings, I carried on chatting with Carrie about this book.

"What are we talking about?" Luke asked.

"My book, I'm just filling Carrie in!" I responded as we walked along. I had already told Luke all about it last week over lunch.

"Oh, the book about a bunch of lesbians?" he asked with a snicker.

I squinted my eyes at him and tilted my head. I looked at his face under the glow of the street lights, studying his expression. I tried to figure out how he had concluded that my book was "about a bunch of lesbians" from our previous conversation. I had told him was that I was going to write about women in the Outdoor Industry. Luckily for Luke, we reached the front door of our destination before I had a chance to respond to his comment, and we didn't run into each other for the rest of the night.

* * *

Luke's comment was upsetting, but not because he labeled women in the outdoors "lesbians." I don't see that specific label as insulting at all. His comment was upsetting because it insinuated that only women of a certain identity enjoy outdoor activity and work in the outdoors. He has a strict stereotype about women in the outdoors, and *that* is the problem.

I know Luke's mindset is not unique. Many people have varying stereotypes about women who work in the outdoors or enjoy an outdoor hobby. This outlook is disconcerting because it makes women feel like they don't belong in the Outdoor Industry if they don't fit a specific mold or fulfill one of those stereotypes. Luke's casual "joke" prompted me to think more critically about society's social perception of the female outdoor athlete and how that perception impacts the female experience. When Luke imagines a woman who is passionate about working in the outdoors, he visualizes one specific stereotype. How common are these limiting stereotypes, really?

* * *

Several women I had spoken to talked about this trend. They shared that society has constructed several distinct categories for the "types of women" who enjoy the outdoors. This gendered process of categorization (that all too commonly exists in other industries) limits women that don't fit into one of the boxes for each "type" of female outdoor enthusiast. When women don't feel like they embody or can live up to the society's stereotypes, women feel like they don't belong in the outdoor community. Studies show that this feeling of belonging is extremely important to women, and when they don't feel this way, they are far less likely to participate in outdoor activity. If they do end up participating in outdoor activity, they often do so with increased hesitation and a lack of confidence, feeling pressure to prove themselves or earn a sense of belonging. In other words, these stereotypes act as a significant barrier to female participation in outdoor activity.

In Jenna William's paper about the portrayal of females in Outdoor Industry media, she interviewed five women who were active in the outdoors. When the women were "asked to identify differences between themselves and other outdoor enthusiasts, the common response was that they did not feel intense enough…The five women interviewed all have experience in the outdoors and feel outdoorsy, but don't necessarily feel intense enough to fully belong in the outdoor community. They don't fit into the leisurely female category or the hardcore enthusiast category, and it is likely that they are not alone."

When we do see images of and hear stories about women in the outdoors, we are generally made aware of two types of outdoor females: the badass athletes and the beautiful models. The dialogue surrounding female outdoor athletes reinforces the idea that women who are athletic are unique and not representative of average women. These examples are polarizing for many of us, as we don't clearly fit into either category. I'm not saying these women shouldn't be showcased in outdoor media—they absolutely should. Instead, I am arguing that we need to broaden the definition of the outdoorswoman to include females of varying skill levels and differing physiques. Every woman should be exposed to relatable examples of female participation in the outdoors.

* * *

Katie Harper is a student at Georgetown and currently works as an outdoor education guide at the university. During our interview, I asked her what it is like to be actively involved in the outdoor education program at Georgetown.

She laughed and said, "When I tell my roommates stories about my outdoor escapades, they tend to laugh at me. I'm not offended, though. They really don't mean any harm... they just aren't understanding when it comes to that kind of thing. They can't relate to it."

When I asked her to elaborate, she continued, saying, "When I refer to my latest excursion, I get comments like, 'Oh yeah Katie could totally be a lesbian. She loves camping and stuff.' Which is just kinda like, okay...So I don't talk about [my outdoor interests] much with my friends anymore."

Katie has found that it's easier to avoid talking about the outdoors with her friends, altogether. It's too bad that she doesn't feel like she can talk about her passion with the people who care about her most. Katie and I sat together for about half an hour and for a good portion of that time, we talked about how limiting our friends' perceptions of the female outdoor athlete are.

I agreed with her, saying, "My friends call me 'crunchy' when I get excited about an upcoming hike or something having to do with nature. They're my dear friends and I know they would never purposefully say anything to hurt me so we just laugh it off together. But it has always bothered me a little that my interest in the outdoors automatically makes me the crunchy granola-loving hippie."

We both agreed that these specific stereotypes society has formed are restrictive and deter many women from feeling like they have a place in the outdoors. We asked the question: Why isn't there enough room in the outdoors for girly-girls and tomboy-girls, for lesbian women and straight women, alike?

It seems that college-aged kids have a slim definition of a woman who enjoys the outdoors, and think it's funny to joke about the girls who don't fit into that definition. These jokes strengthen the gendered expectations that permeate the social sphere of the Outdoor Industry.

* * *

It makes sense that our society has labeled the Outdoor Industry as man's environment and has consequently (and erroneously) projected the idea that tomboy-masculine girls are the most successful in the outdoors. After all, we associate the same traits with masculinity and the outdoors: strength, courage, power, force. These typically masculine characteristics are what we have been conditioned to deem as necessary for success in the outdoors (consciously or subconsciously), and therefore it seems that the rugged outdoors is a place made for rugged men.

Dr. Britian Scott, professor of psychology at the University of St. Thomas, echoed this sentiment, saying: "For women who are participating in wilderness experiences, relying on their bodies to connect with nature can be a mind-blowing experience. But you have to get there first...There are still differences in the way we socialize girls and boys. Our culture continues to define femininity in ways that put women at odds with their natural self so that it's difficult to adhere to the feminine ideal and use your body effectively in the natural world."[25]

Sarah Barker, a freelance writer from St. Paul commented on Dr. Scott's work, saying: "Scott's work shows that the way women are encouraged to look and act 'alienates women from their natural bodies and limits women's nature-embedded experiences.' For example, she asked a roomful of men and women if they owned clothing or shoes that made it impossible to run or climb. All of the women raised their hands. She gave the example of a group of men and women on a month-long wilderness trip and asked if they would emerge from

---

25 [i] Barker, Sarah. "Empowering Women in the Outdoors: Why the White-Hot Interest?" Star Tribune, Star Tribune, 29 June 2017, www.startribune.com/ women-in-the-outdoors-x2009-why-all-the-white-hot-interest/431595953/.

the experience looking more feminine or more masculine. Dirtier, less-groomed, hairier, stronger? All masculine traits."[26]

Just for kicks, I Googled synonyms for "manly" and "feminine." The synonyms for "manly" were listed as brave, courageous, bold, valiant, fearless, macho, intrepid, daring, heroic, adventurous, strong, muscly, rugged tough, powerful. The synonyms for "feminine" were listed as ladylike, soft, dainty, female, tender, womanly, womanish. This set of gender expectations is deeply entrenched in our society. As a result, our culture only accepts a few specific female stereotypes as belonging in the outdoors. These stereotypes commonly include the granola-crunchy lesbian, the badass girl athlete who kicks the guy's butts, and the flirty athletic girl who turns the guys' heads. I am not arguing that these women don't exist, as many female outdoor enthusiasts do in some way represent these descriptions. All the power to them! We may all embody these stereotypes to different degrees, depending on the day.

I am arguing that there are so many different "types" of women who enjoy the outdoors, that women shouldn't be categorized into "types" at all.

* * *

26 Barker, Sarah. "Empowering Women in the Outdoors: Why the White-Hot Interest?" Star Tribune, Star Tribune, 29 June 2017, www.startribune.com/women-in-the-outdoors-x2009-why-all-the-white-hot-interest/431595953/.

Do these distinct categorizations encourage women to alter their personality and change their behavior in order to belong?

Jamie Anderson, a professional snowboarder and the gold medal winner in the 2014 Olympic freestyle event, put it best when she said, "I just knew nice always had to be tough! I grew up a tomboy so I've always tagged along with the boys!" When I read this quote, I smiled because having grown up as a tomboy myself, I related to this sentiment. Upon reflection, I realized that this seemingly simple quote points to the limitations our society places on the female athlete.

As she stated, Jamie's natural affinity toward being a tomboy may have led to her successful inclusion into the snowboarding community, and that's a positive thing for Jamie and other women like Jamie. However, the idea that "nice has to be tough" and life is easier in outdoor athletics if you are a tomboy is extremely limiting for women who do not embody this identity. Women should not have to "perform gender" to belong. This quote showcases the unfortunate assumption that in order to be a successful athlete in the outdoors, women often have to sacrifice their femininity and blend in with the guys.

Kim Kircher echoed this idea in her interview, saying that when she first began her work in the ski patrol industry, she would tie her hair up in a bun under her helmet, and would attempt to look like one of the guy ski patrollers. She took it as a compliment when people thought she was a man from afar. She knew she would be seen differently if she was seen as a female ski patroller.

Kim mentioned that as she has aged, she has begun to understand that she need not sacrifice her femininity in order to belong in her industry and do her job well. She told me that she now braids her hair and ensures that it sticks out of her ski helmet when she is on the job. She is proud of her gender.

Kim stated that improvement will come for the female athlete when society accepts women who lie outside of these prescribed roles as outdoor athletes. She pointed out that women in outdoor sport have so much more to offer than what is allowed when they try to sublimate themselves and fit into the boundaries that have already been set out. These boundaries limit a woman's performance by discouraging her from acting in a way that is natural to her for fear of not "belonging." Kim had summed it up by saying that we need to "try to get away from those railroad tracks that tell everyone who they are and what they have to do." These "railroad tracks" tell women in the outdoors who they are. Women are told they are "manly" or they are "tomboys."

* * *

Moona Whyte echoed this sentiment in her interview, telling

me: "I recently graduated from college…but people keep asking me, 'are you going to get a job?' I've been kiting and competing for a few years now. I'm trying to make money through my sport and follow the path of my dad, some of my friends, and my boyfriend who have been able to make a living through sponsors' support. It's a little annoying that no one asks my boyfriend if he's going to get a job. Even if they are being completely reasonable, it makes me feel like it's expected/accepted that I, as a girl, wouldn't be able to make a living through my sport."

Moona provided the perfect example of an instance when our societal "railroad tracks" tell women in the outdoors what they have to *do*. Our general population seems to think that a female athlete should still get a "real" job, build a family, and settle down because this is what women do, right?

Cori Coccia, an experienced solo-hiker and outdoor educator, mentioned she has faced similar expectations. She shared that there are many limiting stereotypes for outdoor educators— specifically for female outdoor educators. She said, "female outdoor educators face the expectations that they should 'do it all'…they seem to be expected to have children and continue to follow the traditional trajectory other women do."

Women not only face boundaries in who they *should be* in the outdoors. They also face expectations about what they should *do* outside of the outdoor activity. These boundaries and expectations are unique to women and negatively impact their outdoor experience.

* * *

After talking with Kim, I also realized that I, too, have attempted to minimize my femininity in the past when I have partaken in traditionally masculine activities. When I go to lift weights at the YMCA in my neighborhood, I always tie my hair up and wear my most basic unisex t-shirt. I have never planned this out with conscious reasoning, but I realize now that my desire to appear as if I belong in a room full of guys has played into my outfit decisions and my overall gym experience.

This realization brought me closer to understanding the complexity of this barrier to female participation in the outdoors. It is easy to say that this barrier will break down if women abandon their desire to conform to these stereotypes and own their individuality. However, this barrier is bigger than a change in the female's perspective and calls for a multifaceted, large-scale solution. Women often feel as if they aren't given a choice but to conform to a specific stereotype. Unfortunately, conforming in certain ways often allows a woman to advance her skills or her career in a way that would be impossible otherwise. We need to examine the big picture and reorient what traits our society values in the outdoors.

The eighteen women I interviewed are each unique in their own ways. They vary widely in their age, experience level, lifestyle, and personality traits. It is clear that these women did not conform to society's limiting expectations. Instead, they stayed true to their identity and have created their own paths despite these limits we are so painfully aware of. They have shown me that I need not pay attention to these limits. And neither do you.

7

LET'S CRUNCH
THE NUMBERS

August 2015, Age 19. Junior Sailing Center, The Rochester Yacht Club, Rochester, NY.

I dropped my lifejacket on the lawn and plopped down beside it with a sigh of relief. I leaned back on my tired arms and stretched my legs out on the grass in front of me, pointing and flexing my feet. It felt euphoric to have freed my toes from my wet sneakers and wiggle them around in the warm August breeze.

It was almost a quarter after four and the work day was supposed to be over, but three of my sailors were still waiting for their parents to pick them up. I watched with a smile as the twelve-year-old boys stood by the picket fence, clothes still wet and lunchboxes in hand, arguing about who was taller. From my vantage point, it was clear that Johnny had the height advantage, but I was exhausted after a long day of coaching, and I knew it was best for me to keep out of it.

I looked up into the sunlight, as Paul, my friend and coworker, came over and sat down beside me. He sighed as he took off his sunglasses and began to wipe them off with his shirt. He let out another long, dramatic sigh and I laughed and gave him a pat on the back.

"Yeah, long day," I said, offering to clean his glasses on my cotton sleeve after watching him try and fail to do so with the sleeve of his tech t-shirt.

"Thanks," he said passing them over to me. "Yeah, I really thought that wind was going to lighten up. I'm surprised it still hasn't. We spent more time swimming today than sailing. Are you still up for joining us for our afternoon session?"

I passed his sunglasses back to him and took a deep breath in, contemplating if I wanted to get back out on the water in my own sailboat, a Laser I had bought at the end of last summer. A few of the guys and I usually tried to get out after work on Thursdays, but today had felt especially long and the breeze was still blowing at about twenty-five knots with big waves rolling in from the north. It was great training weather as we didn't get many breezy days on Lake Ontario. I needed to learn how to get more comfortable in these conditions, but with each passing minute reclining on the grass, it was more tempting to drive home and get my sunburnt body back to the safety of the suburbs.

"Yeah, I'm up for it," I said with a long exhale. I reached into my lifejacket pocket and pulled out the granola bar that I hadn't had time to eat before lunch. I knew I was going to need it.

Twenty minutes later, after the last parents had come and gone with their same weekly explanations for their tardiness, I started rigging my boat. Paul had finished rigging and was putting on his gear beside me.

"Mar, can I help you step your mast?" he asked, watching me piece together the upper and lower portions of the mast before feeding it into the sail. "It can get kind of sketchy in this wind, you know…"

"Thanks, but I'm good," I responded not looking up but concentrating on aligning my sail. "I got it."

Once I had pulled the entire sail onto the mast, I lifted the mast with focus and used all my strength to muscle it upward with my shoulder, not letting it touch the ground. The sail flapped violently against the resistance of the wind and I had to fight the breeze until the mast was perpendicular to the hull. With the mast finally upright, I inched my body closer to the hull and attempted to place it into the Mast Step, the small hole that the mast sits in, in a controlled manner. My body pumping with adrenaline, I stood back to make sure the sail looked straight. Paul and a few of the other guys looking on let out a few cheers and a half-hearted round of applause.

"Yeah, yeah, thank you..." I said with a smile and a shake of my head. I quickly wrapped up the rest of my rigging and jogged into the bathroom to put on my gear. Trading in my shorts and t-shirt for a neoprene suit and my sneakers for rubber boots, I scrambled back out to my boat and wheeled it to the launching dock. The last of the boys had just launched, and I looked out at their five boats circling around in the river basin, waiting for me to hit the water.

"Now or never, Mar," I thought, as I took one deep breath and pushed the bow of my boat into the water.

I pushed off the dock and felt my sail fill with power as I headed toward the circling boats. "This is why I love this sport," I thought as a gust of wind propelled me forward. I felt like I was flying.

When I reached the group, Paul nodded and attempted to yell

over the breeze, saying: "Alright, boys, how about we head out and do a long upwind and then work our way back down? Try to make it in before dinnertime!"

We agreed and we were off, sailing upwind between the piers toward the lake. As soon as we moved past the shelter of the river tree line, we began to move quickly, and the boys stopped joking around with each other. As we neared the lake, the waves got bigger and our boats began to separate. I was feeling good, leaning backward and fully hiking off the side of the boat. I felt like I was in a groove, working my sail and my body with the waves. Paul was leading the group, and our pack attempted to stay close together, working our way through the steep waves toward the north.

After about forty-five minutes of grueling upwind sailing, I saw Paul slow his boat up ahead. Our pack had separated pretty significantly, and I found myself in the middle of the group. My quads and biceps burned, but I was proud of my sailing. We had been going pretty fast. It was time to head back downwind. We circled up, waiting for the last of our group to reach us, and we turned downwind.

The downwind leg is the most fun in big breeze. It's pretty exciting to ride the waves and to maximize speed, feeling the power of the wind propelling you forward. There's not a lot of stability when sailing a Laser downwind in big breeze.

The fastest sailors push their boat to sail by the lee, meaning they choose a risky angle closer to the wind direction, and transition from angle to angle as they slice through the waves.

We flew down the lake. There was nowhere to hide from the strength of the wind and the water; it surrounded us for as far as we could see. I felt myself disappear between two waves, and for a moment I was held captive in a room with walls made entirely of water. I had no time to make an escape plan as those waves were moving on whether I was ready to or not. I could vaguely hear the guys yelling over the wind, taunting each other to push their boats further to the edge.

It is common for Laser sailors to capsize in heavy breeze (at least among a crowd of our medium-ranged skill level). When one of the dudes in our group capsized, we stopped and circled together to wait as he swam to his boat and righted it. One of the other guys would usually sail over and check-in with him to make sure he was all good. As our group sailed and stopped and sailed and stopped, I was hanging in the back, choosing the relatively safer angles and focusing more on survival than speed. I could have (and should have) let my boat go and fly over the crest of the next wave, but something held me back.

Upon reflection, I realize that I was giving myself a cop-out excuse. I didn't push myself because no one had told me I should. I knew I could keep up with these guys, but I was afraid to take that risk. Even though I didn't consciously let it affect me, I was the only girl among five guys, and that affected my sailing. I didn't want to be *that girl* who capsizes. I was aware that I was the token girl in our group, and I wanted to prove that a girl could "hang." For some reason, the image of the five dudes pulling back to wait for me to swim to and right my boat seemed like more of a big deal than us waiting for one of the guys to do the same. I didn't want to be the one to slow the group down.

At that moment, I wasn't thinking about my gender. I was just thinking about playing it safe. I just wanted to show that I belonged. It was more important to me to make sure that my presence among them wasn't a big deal than it was to push myself to get better at my sport. I wonder if there had been three guys and three girls if I would have felt these same inhibitions? Though it's possible, I don't think I would have. I think I would have been more encouraged to push myself and to take that risk.

* * *

In her thesis paper, *The Gendering of Outdoor Recreation: Women's Experiences on Their Path to Leadership*, Mary Ellen Avery (Texas State University, 2015) shared that there is a significant gender discrepancy in outdoor recreation activities, and while female participation numbers are beginning to grow, they still significantly lag behind male numbers. The Outdoor Industry is dominated by men, and my conversations with athletes in the field support that assertion. This difference in gender population size has several negative effects on the female experience in the outdoor community.

The small number of female participants in the outdoor community allows for the continued acceptance of gender bias in the outdoor community. It's a cycle. Fewer females in adventure sports leads to increased pressure placed on the women within the sport because all eyes are on them to represent the abilities of the female population. This increased pressure raises the stakes. It also leads to increased discomfort within the outdoor community and discouragement, on a woman's part, to take the risks necessary to advance her skills.

The increase in risk avoidance also slows a woman's learning process. When women take fewer risks, they make fewer mistakes, and athletes need to make mistakes to learn from them. When a woman's learning process is slowed in this way, it takes her longer to reach her full athletic potential, if she is able to at all. This, in turn, leads women to be seen as inferior and less skilled, overall.

Together, the perception that women are inferior and this added pressure make outdoor sport less attractive to women. Understandably, women might not want to face the extreme pressure associated with trying to make it as an elite female athlete in the outdoors. Because of this, fewer women participate at a high level. Because of this, fewer women devote their time to outdoor sport, and the cycle continues.

* * *

In the Outdoor Industry Association's 2016 report on "Outdoor Recreation Participation," gender distribution in the industry was reported as 54 percent male 46 percent female. While these numbers don't appear that alarming, I find this statistic too vague to be comforting. The report doesn't depict the nature of the outdoor activity in which those surveyed participate and neglects to mention level and intensity of participation. We are not given parameters for what it means in this survey to "participate" in outdoor recreation, and therefore this data is difficult to interpret. I am calling for a more detailed analysis of gender in participation in different activities and at different levels of intensity in those activities.

Kendra Stritch, a professional ice climber, supports this idea and believes women's participation in outdoor activities is a matter of degree. She sees women participating outdoors at a recreational level, but said: "It's when you get to the competitive level, women in leadership roles, women guiding and setting ropes, and in riskier sports, that the numbers really drop off."[27]

* * *

October 2016, Age 21. Starbucks Wisconsin Avenue, Washington, DC.

I looked down at my watch: 10:26 a.m. I still had plenty of time. I took a deep breath and took off my jacket, tying it around my waist. As I waited in line, I shifted my weight from foot to foot, swaying to the soft Starbucks song and trying to calm my nerves. I was meeting Adriene Levknecht, a professional kayaker and one of the most skilled paddlers in the sport. I was about a half hour early, but eager to grab a table and set myself up.

I had reached out to Adriene after reading about her racing successes and her inspiring athletic career. I was enthused when I saw her response pop up in my inbox a few minutes after I had sent her a note. It was relatively unusual for me to receive a rapid response from the women I reached out to interview, which is understandable given their busy lifestyles and their logistically challenging locations. (One woman was unable to respond because she was busy stalking elk in the

---

27 [i] Barker, Sarah. "Empowering Women in the Outdoors: Why the White-Hot Interest?" Star Tribune, Star Tribune, 29 June 2017, www.startribune.com/women-in-the-outdoors-x2009-why-all-the-white-hot-interest/431595953/.

mountains, another because she was traversing a glacier.) I was amazed when Adriene told me she was traveling to DC in the next few weeks to visit her sister and would be happy to carry out our interview in person. I couldn't believe my luck!

I found a table toward the back of the coffee shop and sent Adriene an email telling her that I was the blond girl wearing a brown fleece. I pulled out my accounting homework to pass the time but found myself excitedly looking up every time someone walked in the door. After spending about fifteen minutes reading and rereading the same homework problem, I opened my laptop to look into Adriene's kayaking career. I knew from my prior research that she was really good at kayaking—her name kept surfacing when I googled women in the sport—but that's about all I knew.

When I saw the video footage of her kayaking, I was floored. I saw her flipping her kayak around in terrifying rapids as big as an inground pool. I read about the sport, amazed by the intensity of competition. ESPNW had recently published an article that described one of Adriene's typical races, saying:

"At last month's GoPro Mountain Games in Vail, Colorado, about forty pro kayakers, including Levknecht among four women, tackled the Steep Creek Championship on Homestake Creek, a narrow, rocky and extremely steep body of whitewater tucked into a deep ravine that starts at around nine thousand feet

and drops nearly five hundred feet over one mile. Resembling a series of mini waterfalls, the creek's rock ledges have names like Leap of Faith.

In these events, each athlete attempts to paddle from start to finish as fast as possible, many bonking off the rocks like pinballs, and some capsizing when they're spun around and knocked backward over the ledges. When their boats momentarily disappear under the bubbling water and surface bottom up, there is a split second of panic among the spectators. Rescuers lining the creek lunge toward the area with ropes and poles, but then a head and a paddle pop up and everyone takes a deep breath."[28]

After gaining some insight into the incredibly challenging and exciting nature of her sport, I became even more excited to speak with her in person. I spent a few more minutes surfing the web reading about her successes and I read that Adriene is the greatest female kayaker in the world. Throughout her career, she has won several of the most prestigious races in the sport and was appropriately awarded "Female Paddler of the Year" in 2016 by *Canoe & Kayak.* I was growing increasingly excited (and nervous) to meet her in person.

Adriene and her fiancé, Snowy, walked in about five minutes

28 Farnell, Shauna. "Elite Kayaker Adriene Levknecht's Drive Goes Beyond The Boat." ESPN, ESPN Internet Ventures, 17 July 2015, www.espn.com/espnw/athletes-life/article/13273576/ elite-kayaker-adriene-levknecht-drive-goes-boat.

after 11, and I recognized them right away. Adriene looked just as she had in her pictures, and was still sporting her flip-flops in late October. I smiled and waved from my seat in the back and got up to meet them in line. I was amazed by their friendliness and humility, and my nerves were quickly put at ease.

Snowy left us to run a few errands, and Adriene and I began to run through some of the questions I had prepared. I quickly ditched my question sheet as I learned more about Adriene's background. Our conversation carried us through a wide range of topics, from her love of the sport of kayaking to her dislike of the logistics of wedding planning. I so enjoyed our conversation, and at many points found myself laughing too hard to take notes.

At one point during our interview, Adriene described her favorite annual competition, The Green Race. As I mentioned before, Adriene is the seven-time champion of the Green Race, and currently holds the record for the fastest time down the river. In 2015, the Green Race had 164 entrants, and only seven of those were women. This race is a big deal, and yet females comprised only 4 percent of total entrants. Adriene brought up this difference in gender breakdown and stated that it has a snowball effect. She mentioned that when women are in the minority, each female participant feels as if all the eyes lining the river that day are on her.

She pointed out that women feel as if they are under a micro-scope because if two women crash during the race, that has a huge effect on the crowd's perception of female kayaking. If half the women crash, say three out of five, the kayaking community jumps on the online forums and starts talking badly about female kayakers.

When I asked if the same trend occurs for males, she said no. Even if the same ratio of men crash, it wouldn't have a big effect on the crowd's perception of male kayaking. It seems to me that "male kayaking" is just thought of as kayaking, period. The smaller number of female participants deter women from participating. Adriene mentioned that there are far more women who kayak on the Green River than race on the Green River. She suspected that the women who choose not to race are cautious about harming their reputation.

Gender bias tends to be further justified by this difference between male and female participants, as many assume that the smaller number of female participants means females are not able to compete at a high level. Adriene defeats men with ease and has proven that this is not the case.

Gender bias also occurs when assumptions are made about the entire female population based on the performance of the few women who participate in adventure sports. According to Adriene, there will be a microscope on female adventure athletes "until male and female numbers are equal."

* * *

Females feel this pressure across many adventure sports. Claire Smallwood, a backcountry skier, mentioned that she occasionally feels restrained by her own inhibitions when she skis the backcountry in Chile. In her interview, she shared that when she skis with a group of men (which she mostly does because there aren't a lot of female backcountry skiers in Chili), she hangs back in the back of the pack.

When the rest of the men are hitting the jump or a tricky part of the cliff, she has this internal dialogue going on where she's not sure she should barrel off just like those did before her. She is held back because she doesn't want to be "that girl" who crashes and falls. Instead, she uses that fear as her reasoning to hang back until someone says, "You should do it. Go for it!" If no one says that, she is less likely to go for it, and later regrets it.

Ginger Bruns, an outdoor enthusiast and education guide at Georgetown University, mentioned feeling this added pressure when she participated in the 100 kilometer hike from Washington, DC to Harpers Ferry, Virginia last year. She said that "sometimes in endurance sports, you are worried that you will hold the group back, especially if you are the only girl…you don't want to mess it up."

Both Claire and Ginger articulated the mental processes that tend to inhibit female adventure athletes. I have formed the hypothesis that these thoughts are due in part to the athlete's awareness of her gender and awareness that she is in the minority in her sport. I felt encouraged and motivated when I heard that these internal inhibitions are felt by the greatest athletes in outdoor sport. I also feel inspired to increase the number of women in the outdoors, from the lowest levels of intensity to the highest.

Misadventures magazine recently published an essay that emphasizes the gender disparity and demonstrates how women feel they have to prove themselves when they are outnumbered and "tokenized" as the only woman in an outdoor setting. Katie McDonnell, a student at Elon University and a recent National Outdoor Leadership School (NOLS) graduate, spoke about her experience, saying: "During my time at NOLS, there was a week where I was the only girl in a group of eight. It was part of the ISGE (Independent Student Group Expedition) and I was a little nervous, but at the end of it, I earned a lot of respect from the guys I was traveling with. I worked very hard alongside them and they saw me as an equal, and that was a great feeling!" source

Katie's quote, while inspirational, shows that there is still a perception that women need to *earn* respect from the men before they are seen as an equal. While one could argue that both men and women feel the need to earn respect from their counterparts, it has been my experience that as a girl, you have to work harder than the men around you to prove that you belong. I have limited myself in my athletic activity in the past, and those limits were in my head. I should have pushed my boat to the point where I was uncomfortable. If I capsized, it would have made me a better sailor. If the boys I was sailing with ever thought of me as "the girl" who capsized, that would have been their problem, not mine.

I learned a lot from Adriene, Claire, and Ginger. After speaking with them, it's clear that one direct way to make outdoor sport more appealing to women is to increase female participation in the outdoors, at all levels. If more women participate in outdoor activity, more women will feel comfortable in the outdoors. Increased comfort will lead to increased enjoyment and increased skill. Both of these things will further increase participation of females in the outdoors. This sounds like a snowball effect similar to the one Adriene described. We just need to get the snowball rolling the other way. We have the ability to turn this vicious cycle into a positive cycle.

8

MEN EMPOWERING WOMEN

November 2016, Age 21. College of Charleston Sailing Marina, Charleston, South Carolina

"How have ya been, Maryn?" Jon asked with a friendly pat on my lifejacket. We were sitting on the edge of an inflatable coach boat in Charleston, getting bounced around by the waves and pelted by the rain that was riding the frigid twenty-knot breeze. It was our last women's regatta of the season.

"I've been good, Jon, how about you?" I replied, lifting my chin out from the collar of my jacket. Jon was my high school sailing coach. He had truly inspired my love for the sport, and he had taught me just about everything I knew about sailing.

Jon was all-around one of my favorite people. I was sad to say goodbye to him my junior year when he left to coach at Jacksonville University.

We caught up between races, and I filled him in on this book. He listened attentively and when I was finished explaining the topic, he said, "That sounds awesome. I'm so glad you're writing about that. We're not all monsters, though. So many dudes in the industry are out there dedicating their time to empowering women. Don't forget about us!"

I nodded, looking around the coach boat and over to the dock in the harbor. There were probably ten male coaches standing in the rain. Some passionately giving instructions to their female sailors with dramatic hand motions, others attentively watching the racing through binoculars—only pausing to scribble notes on their wet pad. These were men who were dedicating their lives to advancing women in the sport, and it wouldn't be right to discuss this topic without mentioning them.

* * *

December 2017, Age 22. Home, Rochester, NY

Over our last winter break, specifically during that seemingly never-ending week between Christmas and New Years, my sisters and I found ourselves unable to leave the house due to the blizzard that was waging outside. Seeking entertainment and having already finished two seasons of *Friends,* we sat on the living room floor contemplating our next move.

Our mom walked into the living room, and seeing us spread out like starfish across the rug, she leaned against the door with a hand on her hip. A smile spreading across her face, she asked: "Are you guys looking for something to do?"

My sisters and I glanced at each other, knowing that she would have a chore for us if we answered affirmatively. I rolled over and grimaced, ready to take one for the team. Before I could volunteer, Hannah (the quickest of the three of us) sat up and said: "Actually, we are going to go through the boxes in the attic today. I know you mentioned that there's some cool stuff up there and we'd love to help you organize it."

"Oh, okay! I was going to ask that one of you clean the inside of all the windows but that can wait until tomorrow," our mom replied as she made her graceful exit. After watching her go, Hannah turned around to face us, a proud grin spreading across her face.

"You're welcome," she said with satisfaction, standing up and reaching down to lend me a hand.

"Yeah, yeah," I said as I felt a smile involuntarily spreading across my face. I grabbed her hand and jumped up. "There better be something exciting for us up there."

Three hours later, the attic delivered. We were sitting cross-legged on the attic floor, bundled in our warmest sweaters and wool socks and surrounded by old yearbooks and photo albums. Unlike my sisters, I don't have a strong memory of my middle school years. For better or for worse, my sisters act as my childhood memory bank, shamelessly basking in the enjoyment that comes from reminding someone of her [mortifying] middle-school mishaps.

"Oooh remember this Maryn-phase?" Hannah asked, flapping a photo in front of me, an amused grin spreading across her face once more.

I squinted my eyes and tried to snatch the picture from her as she yanked it away. She giggled as she leaned back on her elbows and held it up to the light bulb hanging from the ceiling beam. I scooted myself beside her and laid back, peering up at the picture of a proud twelve-year-old Maryn attempting to look natural leaning against a goal post, soccer ball resting on her hip.

"What phase?" I asked, somewhat defensively.

"Your soccer star phase!" she said, handing me the photo. "I'm sure Dad remembers that phase…he was out in the backyard with you every day, tossing the ball to you until it got dark."

I smiled at the photo, fondly thinking back to those warm nights spent playing soccer with my dad. Like many little kids, I grew up playing pee-wee soccer and eventually moved toward playing in a competitive travel league. Around age twelve, I fell in love with the sport and decided I was going to play soccer in the Olympics. The day I made that decision, I ran home from the bus stop and sat in the kitchen, eagerly waiting until our dad got home to share the news. Before he had both feet in the door, I jumped up and eagerly told him of my life plan. Completely serious, he put on his game face and nodded, saying, "Alright, Mar. Let's do this."

In hindsight, my dad's support is amazing to me. I was a middle-school-aged girl and he was a basketball player with no soccer experience, but every night for the following months, he played in the backyard with me after his long day of work. He took my dream seriously and he genuinely believed in me. His support has always made me feel like I could do anything.

Three years later, after an ankle fusion and several knee injuries, I found myself limping off the field more days than not. I spent my off-days icing my foot on the couch, passing on outings to the mall with my friends for fear that walking too much would irritate my ankle. I distinctly remember the day the doctors told my dad and me that I needed to seek other athletic outlets—particularly ones that don't involve running. After a tear-filled ride home, I told my dad we needed to get a second opinion. My heart ached when instead of assuring me as he usually did, he slowly shook his head and with a pained look in his eyes, said: "We'll figure this out together."

* * *

The following summer, I decided to sign up for a week-long "learn to row" camp offered by my high school. It was the summer before my freshman year, and it just felt right. A competitive, running-free, sport that favors tall girls? Sign me up. I showed up at the river on the first day full of enthusiasm and eager to get on the water. By the end of the week, my hands were torn up and my enthusiasm had dissipated. While I could see the beauty in the sport (and have *so* much respect for rowers), I didn't enjoy the long days of monotonous motion and I realized that crew wasn't for me.

A few weeks later, during the fall of my freshman year, I noticed signs hanging in our high school promoting our high school sailing team. I stopped to read the poster more carefully, trying to remember every detail. They were holding a "learn-to-sail" program this week after school. Intrigued, I brought it up at dinner that night.

"Maryn! You have to do this!" my dad exclaimed with genuine excitement, "This could be it for you! It's outside, it's
competitive…it's a lifelong sport…" Our family didn't know
anything about sailing and had never stepped foot inside the
Yacht Club's gates, but there wasn't a question in his mind
that I could do it. Excited by my dad's excitement, I decided
to give it a go.

* * *

Eight years later, lying on the ground of the attic surrounded
by old photos and memories, I was filled with a deep sense
of gratitude for my dad. I thought back on the moments that
weren't pictured, like those summer nights when he would
take my sisters and me to the biggest hill in our neighborhood
(which we aptly named "Big Mama"—not to be confused with
the similarly steep but less intimidating "Little Sis"). We would
line up at the bottom, still shaky without our training wheels
and he would cheer us on as we slowly attempted to ride up
the hill. He would walk behind us, and we felt comforted by
the fact that just before we started to roll backward, he would
be there to catch us by the bike seat and would muscle us up
to the top.

Our dad not only supported us in our athletic and outdoor
pursuits, he genuinely believed in us. After sitting on the coach
boat with Jon in Charleston, I realized that the confidence he

gave us has shaped how my sisters and I view ourselves in the outdoors and in life. We are one lucky bunch.

* * *

Many women who have successfully incorporated outdoor activity into their lifestyle have been inspired, supported, and encouraged by men that empower women. Kate Taylor, a fly fishing guide in Alaska and Oregon, successfully founded her own adventure travel company. She told me, "I've been fortunate to have received mentorship and support along my entire fishing journey from men of all ages and levels. These generous souls far outweigh any negative experiences I may have received from anyone biased against me due to gender."

Her words reminded me of the anecdotes I collected for this book. When ski patroller Kim Kircher was disrespected by the man she was supposed to be saving, her male coworker, Brent stood up for her. Brent defended her when he did not have to, and showed that his respect for her was greater than the injured man's ignorance.

Kim also spoke highly of her boss, Paul. She said that he "has always been an outlier, in terms of hiring women [in the ski patrol industry]." She said that 20-30 percent of their crew has always been women, and that is an extremely high percentage for the industry. Paul made it clear that he valued female patrollers for their judgement and their logical decision making processes. Because of Paul's support, Kim has never felt sexism on her crew.

* * *

Similarly, when Adriene Levknecht's acquaintance asked if she was going to "run shuttle," Adriene's partner Snowy defended her. He replied with gusto and said that Adriene wasn't there to run shuttle, and she would likely run more rapids than him. Snowy stood up to his own friend in defense of Adriene and her abilities.

Adriene also mentioned that one of the strongest influences in her successful kayaking career was her mentor, Shane Benedict. When Adriene first decided to chase her passion for kayaking, she moved to North Carolina and lived in Shane's basement. He supported her passion and encouraged her to pursue kayaking as a career. Adriene said she owes a lot of her success to him and will forever be grateful for his support.

* * *

This past September, I witnessed a moment that showcased how supportive men can be in the face of gender bias. It was a beautiful fall afternoon on the Potomac, about sixty-five degrees and sunny. The breeze was moderately strong, and it was Thursday, which meant it was race day for our sailing team. College sailing is very competitive, and our race days are often intense.

Competitive sailing involves racing around a course marked by buoys floating in the water. There are two people in each boat, and one person steers while the other maintains boat balance, feeds information to the skipper, and controls the smaller sail. There is a lot of tactical strategy involved and a great deal of athletic skill is necessary (especially in dinghy sailing). Each race begins with all of the boats lining up (or attempting to line up) underneath an invisible line drawn between two buoys perpendicular to the wind.

The start of the race is often one of the most difficult parts. You can't make a sailboat stop and go on demand, you're always moving, and the wind is always shifting. Exact timing is crucial and extremely difficult to achieve.

That sunny Thursday, the whistles were blown for the last race of the day, and I was subbed out to sit on the coach boat. As usual, the last race was just for fun, and no scores were ever recorded. One of my friends, Esther, who was new to the team, had taken over the tiller and was skippering her first race.

The start was a few seconds away, and I watched as Esther sailed into the starting area very slowly. As she approached the line, she fouled another boat, tapping the other boat's hull lightly while she was on port. The boy steering the other boat, Adam, whipped around, put his hand on the bow of her boat, and vehemently thrust her boat backward. He yelled loudly at her for hitting him. Adam's action was so aggressive that her boat rocked backward, sending a wake off the sides.

I looked on in shock. Sailors keep their hands to themselves in racing. No one ever has reason to touch another person's boat, let alone push it back three feet.

My coach, Jim, was also amazed by this poor display of sportsmanship. I looked over at him and saw him looking on with an expression of disbelief. He motored over to Adam's boat and told him how absolutely unacceptable his actions were. Jim sent Adam into the dock and told him to apologize to Esther (who looked near tears) on his way in.

As the boys sailed by Esther's boat, I heard a meek and softly spoken, "Sorry, Derek."

I was confused for a split second until I realized that Derek was Esther's crew. "Oh," I thought sarcastically, "They are apologizing to the boy in the front of the boat, the boy who was along for the ride...makes perfect sense."

As I witnessed Adam apologize to the boy of the boat when

he had more directly wronged the girl, I knew that this event wasn't simply about poor sportsmanship. Gender had played a role in Adam's complete lack of respect for Esther. I can't seem to picture Adam and his crew treating a boy in the same way he treated Esther. His reaction to her foul had showcased his lack of respect for her as a competitor and his lack of an apology to the person he actually wronged showcased his lack of respect for her as a person.

I looked back at Jim, trying to see if he had heard Adam apologize to Derek. From his expression, it was clear that he had.

"Did I just hear what I think I heard?" he asked, tapping the steering wheel with his index finger. "That's not right. We need to do something about that."

* * *

At first when I witnessed that event, I was upset. I didn't understand how a teammate could treat another teammate so poorly. However, upon reflection, I have realized that this story has more good than bad, especially if one considers my coach's actions.

Although only a handful of people had witnessed Adam's actions, Jim addressed the situation soon after practice and set the precedent that this type of bias was not acceptable.

He spoke to Adam immediately after practice and told him to go help Esther put her boat away. Jim not only prevented surface-level mistreatment on that day. In the following weeks, he continued to show us that this type of behavior wasn't acceptable in sailing. The following week at our team meeting, Jim spoke about sportsmanship at all levels and the importance of respecting our competitors.

* * *

As I sat writing this chapter, I realized how grateful I am for the men who have encouraged my love of the outdoors and outdoor sport. Although there is still room for improvement in the way some men treat women in the outdoors, many men are working to empower women and make positive change. These men provide strong role models for us, showing that the first and most crucial step to eliminating biased treatment is recognizing when it occurs. This recognition requires critical eyes, as biased treatment has become the norm in many outdoor contexts. Once the bias is recognized, real and sustainable progress requires courage and commitment. Jim not only confronted Adam directly at the time of the bias, he continued to ensure that this bias didn't continue for the rest of the season. Unprompted, he voiced the importance of unbiased treatment in our team gatherings and encouraged the rest of the team to come to him with any concerns. Jim, and many other women and men like him, are paving the way for change in the Outdoor Industry.

PART 3

PROGRESS

She believed she could, so she did.

—R.S. GREY

9

THE POWER OF A ROLE MODEL

I have experienced my most formative moments perched on the center wooden thwart of my great-grandma's cedar strip racing canoe. After an estimated thousand cumulative hours in that canoe, I feel as if that thwart has been molded especially for my behind and waits all winter for our reunion at the start of the summer.

I learned to paddle shortly after I learned to walk. It took several years before I was strong enough to take a canoe out on my own, but I worked hard at improving my paddling skills and I got stronger every summer. We mostly paddle at our lake house, which is on a small granite rock in the middle of the Stony Lake, in Ontario, Canada. Given the fact that our extended family of twelve only has one 9.9 horsepower tin motorboat, the three canoes sitting at the end of our dock offer a very practical form of transportation. In many cases, they also offer the most reliable form of freedom.

My relationship with that canoe has changed over my twenty-two summers on Stony Lake. My sixth summer, I discovered the thrill of a Canadian Canoeing Regatta. There are two main canoeing regattas on our lake every summer, and they are steeped in tradition and historic familial competition. There is significant prestige associated with regatta success, and thus these events are taken seriously. Our family, neighbors, and old family friends begin training in May and bring our A-game come regatta season. At age six, I broke onto the competitive canoeing scene as more of a passenger than a participant, gingerly dipping my toddler-sized paddle in the water as my grandma fiercely paddled me through the finish line in the grandparent-and-child race, and my mom powerfully paddled me to the finish in the parent-and-child race. In those tense moments on the starting line, the blurry and fleeting moments flying down the course, and the final moments after we slid through the finish and the canoe slowed, I fell in love with the sport. I don't remember how we did that first year, but I do remember how amazed I was by the strength and grit of my grandma and mom. We flew down the racecourse with ease, leaving several boats of men and their sons in our wake. Comfortably perched behind my grandma and mom,

I decided that someday I was going be like them.

My grandma is a small but mighty woman. She has a strong faith, likes to throw a good party, and doesn't seem to be afraid of anything. For as long as I can remember, she has shuffled my sisters and me toward conquering our fears, encouraging us to leap into the rapids at the bottom of the waterfall saying: "Into the inky blackness! Are we afraid?"

"No!" my sisters and I would respond, clipping our life jackets and grasping for each other's hands as we leaped gleefully into the foaming whitewater.

I spent my next seven summers training for the canoeing regattas, striving to keep up with my grandma when she took her daily paddle around the lake. I worked on strengthening my boat legs and I spent my summer nights counting down the days until I could fly down the racecourse. Being the competitive girl that I am, I often felt too excited and nervous to eat when the morning of the regatta came. I genuinely looked forward to and enjoyed that day, but often felt more relief than remorse after it had passed. Around my fourteenth summer, when my pre-regatta excitement turned into apprehension, I decided my competitive canoeing days were over.

That summer, my grandma, being the supportive and all-knowing woman that she is, brought me to Lockside, the gift shop at the end of the lake. She didn't tell me why she wanted to go, but it's a forty-five-minute boat ride from our cottage, so I knew she had to have a game plan. When we arrived at Lockside, we shut off the motor and tied up our boat about fifty yards from the lock. We climbed the metal ladder up the cement walls of the lock in our bare feet (my grandma doesn't wear shoes in the summer, even when she goes into town), our toes curling around the thin ladder rungs that felt hot from the sun. We made our way into the shop and walked through the rows of hand-crafted wooden furniture into a small back room I had never been in before. I was amazed by what I saw: a small but impressive square room where wooden paddles of every size and grain hung from the walls. My grandma smiled at my awe and gestured to the darker, softer-looking paddles on the wall to our right.

"We're here to get you a new paddle," she said with a pat on the back and a grandma-like grandiose gesture. Wide-eyed, I gave her a tight hug and the held her at arm's length.

"Thank you so much for bringing me here! But we have a closet full of paddles…I've been using that same one for years now and have no complaints." I said, trying to communicate with my eyes that I didn't want her to make a big purchase for me.

"We do have plenty of paddles," she responded, "but you've been using a racing paddle, one with a wider wooden blade built for power. I want you to love paddling for the rest of your life, and now that you aren't so focused on going fast, you need to have a paddle that's built only for enjoyment. I use my mother's thin-bladed paddle for my daily sunrise trip, and I love that paddle more than this lake itself. "

I knew the paddle my grandma was referring to. It was hard not to notice, as it was one of the few paddles we had that was made of dark cherry wood. In the rare moments when my grandma didn't have it with her, it was suspended by a set of nails, hanging above the pile of our paddle inventory. It was well-worn, telling the tale of many miles traveled and showing the signs of many years of love. What I hadn't noticed was the difference in blade size between my grandma's special paddle and the rest of the light-colored paddles resting below it.

"You are one of the strongest paddlers I know, and you don't need to win races to prove that," she continued. "I know that you have a lifetime of canoeing adventures ahead of you. My time on the water made me who I am, and I want the same for you." She had a new sense of pride in her stance and air of defiance in her voice. "So pick one, please! So I don't have to for you."

I went home that day with what quickly became my favorite possession. My cherry wood paddle hangs beside my bed at home in the winter months and travels to the lake with me every summer. It serves as a reminder of my grandma's courage on the water and her faith in me that I too, have that courage.

This past summer, I pushed the canoe off the dock and went out for a paddle at least once a day, putting my special paddle to good use. I enjoyed several tranquil trips paddling through glassy water and often stopped on those days to float and write. I also found irreplicable satisfaction on those days when I pushed off into a strong headwind, felt the bow of the canoe slicing through the choppy water and became attuned to the steady pace of my stroke battling the wind and waves. A few of those nights slipped away from me, and I found myself paddling home in the pitch black after the sunset faded quicker than anticipated. On those nights, I heard my grandma's voice cheering me on, echoing as she cried out: "Into the inky blackness! Are we afraid?"

* * *

In REI's recent survey about the modern female's relationship with the outdoors, they found that six out of ten women were unable to think of an outdoor female role model.[29] While unsurprising, I found this statistic incredibly upsetting. Role models directly influence and shape what a young woman perceives as *possible*. More than just defining these upper

---

29   REI. "2017 National Study on Women and the Outdoors." LinkedIn SlideShare, REI, 30 Mar. 2017, www.slideshare.net/REI_/2017-national-study-on-women-and-the-outdoors.

limits for what is possible, role models directly influence and shape what a young woman perceives as *realistic, practical, and attainable.*

This statistic shows that we have a problem with our media, as modern women are constantly connected to news sources and social channels and only four out of ten are able to recall the name of a female outdoor role model. There is obviously room for improvement in media coverage of female athletes and adventurers—not only on the part of the news and outdoor brand sources but also from the average Instagrammer or Facebook participant. We have a duty to share the successes of our female counterparts and show our friends and followers the exciting things that women are achieving in the outdoors.

This statistic also suggests that some of us might have female outdoor role models in our lives that we do not recognize as such. If had I found myself absent-mindedly filling out the REI survey, it is possible that I might not have recognized the strong role models I have had in my mom and my grandma. Not once have I paused to reflect on the role they have played in shaping my strong relationship with the outdoors and my positive view of myself in the outdoors. As I sat to write this story, I felt a tidal wave of gratitude for the strong women in my life that have shown me that I can do anything I want to do in the outdoors. I have moved throughout my adolescent years feeling proud of myself for being the first person on that hike to leap the divide between the rocks, not recognizing that it was my mom and grandma's contagious confidence and conscious support that have constructed this genuine feeling of self-assurance within me.

REI went on to examine the actual effects of encouragement on young girls and found that highly encouraged girls are more likely to both remain active today and consider spending time outside a "very high priority." They also found that highly encouraged girls place more value on adventure with a significantly higher percentage recognizing "the importance of having excitement/adventure in your life." This data unsurprisingly points to a cyclical trend in encouragement. The women who claimed to be encouraged to spend time in the outdoors were two times more likely to list their mother as their source of encouragement and in turn, were one and a half times more likely to report that it's important to them that their daughter has a relationship with the outdoors.[30]

Christine Norton, an adventure therapy specialist, voiced the serious impact her role models have had on her in a recent interview with *Misadventures*, saying: "My journey [in adventure therapy] started formally when I was nineteen years old and I was a college student. I did an Outward Bound course and one of my instructors was a woman—and actually,

---

30 REI. "2017 National Study on Women and the Outdoors." LinkedIn SlideShare, REI, 30 Mar. 2017, www.slideshare.net/REI_/2017-national-study-on-women-and-the-outdoors.

ironically, her name was Christine, which is my name…I think that makes a difference. When an agency has these women in leadership roles, it's like: "Wow. The Director is a woman." That's awesome because it bursts that glass ceiling. I think it helps me believe in what's possible. What I've noticed about those female trainers and supervisors was that they always gave me a little more than I thought that I could handle. I don't want to say that male supervisors *haven't* done that or *wouldn't* do that, but I feel like when that happens in the field of Adventure Therapy—when women in leadership roles mentor other women by giving them challenges and responsibilities that are just outside of what they think they can handle—I've never grown more."[31]

This past year, AndShesDopeToo and Backcountry.com teamed up to create a documentary titled *Moksha*. *Moksha* showcases three female Nepali athletes who have dedicated their lives to breaking outdoor barriers in their home country. They spend their days mountain biking through the unforgiving Himalayan terrain, determined to spread the joy that comes from getting outside and going on an adventure. A recent article published by Teton Gravity Research reads:

"In Nepal, the overarching societal expectation of young women

---

31   Chambers, Leah. "Interview: Christine Norton, Adventure Therapy
     Specialist." Misadventures Magazine, 9 Dec. 2015, misadventuresmag.com/
     interview-christine-norton-adventure-therapy-specialist/.

is to be nothing more than a married housewife. For Roja, Usha, and Nishma they're not accepting the societal norm. Choosing to fight for gender equity through two wheels, these lady shredders are Nepal's first ever female MBLA certified mountain bike guides and racers...A sport that we often simply see as recreation now serves as a method of freedom for girls in a deeply rooted patriarchal culture, opening the door for sisterhood, upward mobility, and adventure."

'I want to make myself and family proud and let them know I can earn a living by staying and working in Nepal as a woman in the outdoor industry, rather than taking the path chosen by so many youth in my country...to leave, study abroad and never come back.'
—Roja

'After this trip, Roja, Usha and I have become sisters. We now express ourselves openly. We aren't jealous. We are supportive. We ride together. This is important to grow the sisterhood.'
—Nishma"[32]

These women have dedicated their lives to bringing women together and acting as role models for women and girls around the world. They inspire because they not only show serious

---

32 Lozancich, Katie. "How Nepali Women Find Freedom Through Mountain Biking." Teton Gravity Research, 6 Mar. 2018, www.tetongravity.com/video/bike/moksha-finding-freedom-and-empowerment-through-mountain-biking.

athletic skill and expertise, they also show incredible courage and grit.

* * *

Many different types of figures could potentially fall under the term "Role Model." The first thing that comes to mind when a person mentions the term "role model" is frequently a high-profile celebrity. Celebrities are seen as the typical role model because of their wide-spread influence and potential to inspire. While these celebrities can (and often do) yield positive influence, the people we see every day (parents, siblings, friends, coaches, etc.) yield the most lasting influence. These people are capable of personally touching our lives, and we feel a deeper connection with their story.

However, I argue that women need both kinds of role models, the high-profile aspirational figures and the highly accessible supportive figures. There is a necessity for both of these figures because the high-profile celebrity figure has the capacity to show the woman what can be achieved in outdoor sport and the accessible relational figure has the ability to encourage the woman to achieve that success.

It is important that a young woman sees what a woman like her is capable of. An awareness of the accomplishments of the most high-performing female athletes has the potential to inspire confidence in a young woman regarding her own capabilities. And hopefully, that confidence encourages her to set goals without limits. Once a young woman is shown what she can do, it is ideal for her to have a role model that supports her on her path to that goal. This role model should have the ability to encourage the girl within her unique context—to make her dreams feel real and actually attainable. In other words, the first task of a role model is to illustrate the young woman's potential, and the second task is to see to it that she genuinely believes in her ability to reach that potential.

In many cases, these tasks can be achieved by the same person, as these role model figures are not always mutually exclusive. In my experience, my grandma personified both of these types of role models. She not only showed me that it is possible to be a female powerhouse on the water, she also encouraged me to believe that I can be that strong, too. However, it's notable that my grandma did not simply focus on encouraging me to perform at a high level. Her support was dynamic and flexible to my needs and desires. When I was motivated to hone my strength and skills, she trained with me and pushed me to improve. But when my interests shifted and my competitive desires faded, she focused on instilling a lifelong love of the sport. Thank you, Grandma.

1 0

THE ALL-GIRLS EFFECT

January 2014, Age 18. Home, Rochester, NY

Beep! Beep! BEEP!

My stopwatch alarm began to ring, the high-pitched and unforgiving tone entering my consciousness and growing louder with each buzz. I squeezed my eyes and reached out for the watch, promising to myself that I will silence it once and for all and invest in a more encouraging morning alarm. Across the room from me, my twin sister Terese rolled over and let out her daily morning groan. She pulled the covers over her head as I hopped out of bed and knelt down to feel around for my school clothes. I found them over by my dresser and reached for them so I could do a quick smell test.

"Fine enough for me," I thought, as I yanked the polo shirt over my head and pulled on the uniform pants I had dropped on the floor the night before. I pulled my hair into a bun on the top of my head and headed out the door in the dark.

I shut our door quietly on my way out (I'd learned the hard the way that even if she had to get up momentarily, Terese liked to wake herself up on her own terms!) and knocked on our younger sister Hannah's door as I slid to the top of the stairs. Hannah was usually the last one up, but somehow she managed to be the first out the door. I barreled down the stairs to greet our energetic German Shorthaired Pointer and made my way into the kitchen to whip up my favorite meal of the day: Life Cereal.

My sisters and I went to Our Lady of Mercy High School, a Catholic all-girls high school about fifteen minutes from our house. Our mom, an alum herself, worked there as a business teacher and left the house around 6 a.m. every morning. Like my mom, the morning was my favorite part of the day. I put on my tunes and ate my breakfast standing, scrounging through our fridge in an attempt to fill my brown paper bag. No matter how many times we ran to the grocery store during the week, more often than not the best lunch I was able to imagine was PB&J. Slapping my multigrain slices together between bites of cereal, I glanced at the clock. 7:34.

"Terese...Hannah!" I shouted from the bottom of the stairs. I didn't like to feel like I was nagging, but seeing as I hadn't heard any movement and we were late for school two mornings the week before, we had to make moves. Homeroom started at 7:55, and I was not in the mood to be late today. It was quite the scene when the three of us paraded into the main office and had to ask the vice principal (and our mom's best friend) for late passes. Somehow after all this practice, we usually struggled to coordinate our excuses for our tardiness, resulting in a rather unconvincing or simply unfeasible alibi. Although our morning arrival at the main office was met with laughter from our vice principal, our afternoon arrival home was met with scolding from our mom.

I heard Terese's feet hit the ground and Hannah's door swing open. I searched through the coat closet for my warmest jacket and slipped it on, finessing the broken zipper and successfully sealing it up to my chin in preparation for the Rochester, NY wind chill. I pulled on my boots, grabbed the broom, and ran outside to brush the snow off our bright-red two-door Pontiac Grand Am GT. Our uncle had gifted us this car last year, and although we inherited it in its final stages with a few blown out speakers and a permanently illuminated engine light, that sweet little car (which we quickly and aptly named Cherry Bomb) gave us a freedom that changed our lives.

I gingerly turned the key, cranked up the heat, and began to scrape the ice off the front and back windows. I checked my watch: 7:42. That would do, I decided. I ran back into the house and slammed the door behind me in an attempt to alert the sisters of my urgency.

"Let's go!" I yelled, not seeing anyone in the kitchen. Hannah came peeling around the corner, backpack slung over her shoulder.

"I'm ready," she said raising her hands defensively. "Let's go!"

Terese sleepily meandered into the kitchen and popped a bagel in the toaster, completely unconcerned. 7:45.

"Shotgun," I said with a sigh as I grabbed my own bag and slipped out the door. I liked to be punctual, and it was for our own safety that I didn't drive on days like this.

We slid into our spot in the parking lot and the clock on our dash blinked 7:59. All things considered, we had made good time. We piled out of the car and made our way up to the main office, catching the last few minutes of the morning announcements through the speakers in the hallway. We made our way up to the first floor and burst into the front office.

"Good morning, Cannon sisters," our vice principal said with a warm smile, tearing off three late passes from her pad and dramatically setting them down one by one, in front of us.

* * *

A few years removed from high school, I have come to realize that I moved through those years with an unusually high level of comfort and confidence. While the presence of my sisters and my mom and my general familiarity with Mercy High School undoubtedly contributed to this comfort on some level, the all-girls environment shaped the most positive aspects of my high school experience and made me who I am today.

For four years, my friends and I existed in a no-pressure environment. We passed the deodorant around in homeroom, played way too competitively in gym class badminton, and danced our way through the hallways. I didn't feel like I had to conform to a predefined stereotype or seek the approval of anyone around me. I was free to be anything I wanted to be and had the clear opportunity to be whoever that was because every leader, every club president, and every team captain was a girl. I formed deeply genuine and sincere friendships with my classmates and felt supported by other women in a way that I haven't felt since my high school graduation. Given my positive experience, I was surprised when I came to college and even my closest friends looked at me sympathetically when I told them about my high school.

"Oh… I'm sorry," they would respond after I told them that I attended an all-girls school. "That must have been rough… girls are so bitchy."

The first few times I was met by this response, I laughed and changed the subject; but soon those unpleasant conversations prompted me to look into the actual benefits of an all-girls education. I quickly learned that the benefits have been proven through decisive research and I now invite this response, as I enjoy sharing that data with others.

Dr. Myra Sadker summed up my argument succinctly when she said: "When girls go to single-sex schools, they stop being the audience and become the players." 93 percent of girls' school grads say they were offered greater leadership opportunities than their peers at public school, and 80 percent have held a leadership position since graduating from high school.[33] A majority of girls' school grads report higher self-confidence over their coed peers, and one alum noted that in an all-girls setting, increased confidence encourages you to have and meet your own expectations before you aim to meet anyone else's.[34]

* * *

33 "The Power of Girls' Schools." Girls Preparatory School | The Power of Girls' Schools, www.gps.edu/page/why-a-girls-school/the-power-of-girls-schools.

34 "The Power of Girls' Schools." Girls Preparatory School | The Power of Girls' Schools, www.gps.edu/page/why-a-girls-school/the-power-of-girls-schools.

These benefits of an all-girls setting are felt just as strongly, if not more strongly, in the outdoors. Numerous courageous and inspiring women have dedicated their lives to promoting and inviting women to enjoy the outdoors in community with one another. Through their Force of Nature Campaign, REI held over one thousand events designed specifically for women in the 2017-2018 calendar year. These events included wilderness classes, adventure outings, and weekend retreats led by women, for women.

REI's Outessa retreats are three-day immersive retreats, designed to teach, lead, and empower women to explore the outdoors and themselves. Breanna Wilson, a recent Outessa participant, reflected on her experience, saying: "Leaving Outessa you could tell that women had found their tribe. Solo attendees had bonded with other girls in their classes, mother and daughter attendees (and there were a few—even a grandmother and granddaughter duo made an appearance!) were a little dirtier, a little closer, a little more lighthearted than when they arrived. Women tried things they never thought they would—rock climbing, mountain biking—and their enthusiasm for life and the outdoors became apparent, and even contagious by the end of the weekend."[35]

35   Wilson, Breanna. "How REI Mastered The Outdoor, Women-Only Retreat." Forbes, Forbes Magazine, 19 Sept. 2017, www.forbes.com/sites/breannawilson/2017/09/19/how-rei-mastered-the-outdoor-women-only-retreat/#6bce019835fd.

There are numerous outdoor organizations dedicated to bringing women together, including the group AndShesDopeToo. It was founded by an adventurous couple Jennifer and Taylor Killian. I stumbled upon ASDT's Instagram page a few years ago and was immediately inspired by the founding story. "When Taylor Killian was at an end-of-the-year work party in 2013, his colleagues told him how gorgeous Jennifer was. Rather than just agreeing, he immediately said, 'And she's dope, too,' before explaining how she rock climbed, mountain biked, went kayaking and hiked with him."

"And for whatever reason 'and she's dope too,' when I said that, just kind of stuck with me," Taylor Killian said.[36]

ASDT has grown immensely since 2013 and now brings hundreds of women together for their Rendezvous events. More than half of the participants come alone and find companionship and comfort in the women around them. One participant shared her experience, saying: "There's something stirring in all of us. There's an energy in our souls that calls us to come together because there's power in numbers. There's power in knowing and being known, in understanding a bit more of ourselves by learning about others and their stories."[37]

---

36   Christensen, Megan. "'AndShesDopeToo' Empowering Women through Meetups, Clothing."KSL.com, www.ksl.com/?nid=1288&sid=36009839.

37   Megan. "ASDT Rendezvous." The Quirky Climber, 19 May 2017, thequirkyclimber. com/2016/09/15/asdt-rendezvous/.

* * *

It has been my experience that an all-girls environment encourages women to support other women. Kendra Stritch, a professional ice climber, echoed this sentiment, pointing out that the competitiveness that helped her succeed in her sport alienated her from other women. It wasn't until she worked in an all-female environment that she felt connected to other women.

In a recent interview, Stritch said: "I've taught a women's [climbing] clinic for six years now, but I was hesitant at first; I didn't want to teach it… I'm comfortable being the only woman in a group of male climbers, but I never hang out with twelve women. I've never had that many female friends. Women are my competition. I changed my mind after teaching the women's-only clinic. Men will talk over women—they'll 'spew beta'—in a mixed-gender class. I've seen lots of women thrive in an all-female environment."[38]

In addition to increased camaraderie among female athletes, the all-girls environment allows for women to develop their skills faster than they would in a co-ed environment. A recent essay published in *Misadventures* magazine showcases this

---

38 Barker, Sarah. "Empowering Women in the Outdoors: Why the White-Hot Interest?"Star Tribune, Star Tribune, 29 June 2017, www.startribune.com/ women-in-the-outdoors-x2009-why-all-the-white-hot-interest/431595953/.

trend when describing California Women's Watersport Collective, a community of female paddlers. This essay articulates the power of women leading women, saying:

"*Like many outdoor sports, in kayaking you're more often than not the only woman in the group. This isn't a bad thing at all—some of my favorite people to kayak with are male. But this trend does tend to inhibit women's skills development, especially among beginners. 'Generally, being the girl in the group meant being the weak link or the one that the boys had to look out for. The guys were often the ones making decisions and leading down the river,' shares [founder] Melissa.*

Cali Collective seeks to reverse this trend: 'One of our goals is to encourage women to be active leaders—not passive participants—in their paddling group: doing things like getting out front in the rapids, making decisions on the river and assisting in rescues. When women paddle together they have more opportunities do all these things, which gives them more experience and confidence,' Melissa explains.

She also points out, 'women tend to be more honest about their skill set, with both themselves and others. Therefore, I think there's a lot less 'oh you'll be fine' in stepping up to a more challenging run when they may or may not be ready. There's a bit less ego on the water with women and they are often times more supportive and so other women feel less intimidated when learning new skills."[39]

When we harness this power of the all-female environment, we increase the chances that women will jump into a sport, and we also increase the chances that women will stick with that sport. SheJumps, a nonprofit focused on increasing the participation of women and girls in outdoor activities, has made it their mission to encourage women of all ages to "jump in, jump up, and jump out." For women who have never had an opportunity to experience the outdoors, they have events and communities that encourage them to "jump in" to outdoor activity. For women who are looking to get better at what they do, they have events and communities that encourage them to "jump up" in their level of participation. And for women who are currently participating at an elite level, they have events and communities and allow them to "jump out" by acting as a role model and giving back.

There are numerous organizations that, like Cali Collective and SheJumps, see the value in the all-female environment. These organizations have made it their mission to increase the accessibility of all-female learning environments in the outdoors, and we are lucky to be able to take advantage of these opportunities. Overall, one actionable step we can take to eliminate the barriers that women face in the outdoors is

---

39 Zulliger, Laura. "Women on Water." Misadventures Magazine, 20 Nov. 2015, misadventuresmag.com/women-on-water/.

to encourage women to get outside with their girlfriends, and to participate in outdoor sports with other groups of women.

11

WHAT'S THE RECIPE?

———

November 2016, Age 21. Alumni Square Apartments, Georgetown University, Washington, DC.

I leaned against the kitchen wall, feeling the weight of a busy week lift off my shoulders. It was about 5 p.m., and we had just gotten back from one of our last sailing practices of the season. My friend Mac had invited me over for dinner with another one of our teammates, Abby. We laughed while we caught up. We hadn't been able to spend much time together outside of practice this semester. As we chatted over the sizzle of chicken on the stovetop, one of our fellow teammates, Tom, came up. Sitting on the countertop of Mac's small galley kitchen, Abby turned to me and asked: "Did you see me lose it with Tom at practice today?"

I nodded, as my boat had been near Abby's at the time, and I had heard Abby and Tom get into an argument on the race course. Conflict on the race course is not uncommon, given that sailing is a self-policing sport and it's possible for two sailors to have different interpretations of the rules, depending on the situation. Because of this, there is a systematic procedure for protesting the actions of another competitor, and there is never a reason to treat a competitor with disrespect.

Our race-day practices are highly competitive, and therefore these arguments occur somewhat regularly. This argument seemed particularly rough though, and I was on Abby's side.

"Yeah, I did see that," I said. "What happened?"

"I saw it too," said Mac.

"He fouled me, and he didn't even respond when I called him out on it. He was objectively wrong, and Coach told him so after the race. I just can't get over it when he fouls me so blatantly like that and then ignores me!" Abby said.

"Aw…It's all good, he's a good guy," Mac responded, not looking up from the skillet.

"Not to girls on the water," Abby said, leaning forward and swinging her legs. "When we were sailing into the dock, he sailed up next to us and said, 'Don't frown, sweetheart.'"

Mac chuckled, this time turning around. "Yeah but he means well…that's just classic Tom. He's such a good guy… Ya know, it's all good," he said, turning back to stir the chicken.

I looked at Abby, eyes wide. She sighed and pursed her lips. "It's not all good!" I mouthed, shaking my head in amazement.

* * *

I wasn't raised as someone to make excuses—and as I've said, this book isn't an attack on men in the Outdoor Industry. But I'd be remiss if I didn't communicate what I've personally learned and what was shared with me by nearly every successful woman I spoke with in the industry:

Gender bias is a real thing you'll face.

It's snide jokes, it's subtle jabs, it's little things that can drive you nuts (and ruin a perfectly good dinner). And there is no perfect recipe for eliminating gender bias or personally dealing with its effects. But it's also something many women have overcome. These women are paving the way for the next generation of female outdoor professionals like me; like us.

The reality is that if we want to play, we have to be prepared to deal with gender bias. Dealing with it, as I quickly learned, sometimes means attacking the bias straight away, sometimes means ignoring it (for now) to pick your battles, and sometimes means going out and kicking ass on the slopes, waters, skies or whatever location you thrive. That's the amazing thing here. Bias is as much of an opportunity as it is a limitation. Crazy as it sounds, the opportunity to overcome it is part of what the next generation of adventurers can learn from those who came before us.

I believe that standing up to those who promote or allow gender bias is an important step in advancing toward a more equal outdoors. I also have realized that standing up or arguing with those people is an unattractive task. Standing in Mac's kitchen that November evening, I had every opportunity to stand up for Abby and explain to Mac why it's not okay for Tom to treat Abby that way, even if he is a good guy. But I didn't because I did not want to enter into a larger debate about male-female sportsmanship in sailing. I realize now, that I should have mustered my courage and launched into this conversation. These conversations, even if they have the potential to be frustrating, also have the potential to plant the grassroots for change.

* * *

The women I talked to have faced these issues for much longer, and they have probably faced much thornier issues than the ones I've faced in my young career. How have they navigated through these issues?

Given the intricacy of the deeply rooted causes of gender bias in the industry, it makes sense that direct verbal intervention in unjust situations, while essential, is not the single step necessary in our solution. Our solution should be multifaceted and should not be limited to eliminating surface-level bias. Our solution should address the root causes of the unique challenges women face in the outdoors.

Previous chapters showed that encouraging men to take a stake in establishing gender equality in the outdoors, increasing the accessibility of female role models in the industry, and focusing on developing all-female environments are three actionable steps that will improve the female outdoor experience. What other concrete steps should we take to make improvement for women in the Outdoor Industry? Having limited experience in the Outdoor Industry myself, I asked this question to many women I spoke to. I was extremely excited by their answers, as they seemed to outline simple steps that would make an immediate, tangible difference.

When I asked backcountry skier Claire Smallwood what she thought we should do to improve the experience of the female adventurer, she said, "It's actually not that jaw-dropping and insane to see women, unknown women, not sponsored skiers or snowboarders, mountain bikers or climbers, doing phenomenal feats in the outdoors." While she believes in having the top-tier women and their achievements highlighted, there's plenty of room to spotlight "the nurse who gets up every day and goes ski touring before her twelve-hour shift or the mother of five who finds time to go for a trail run three times a week because it clears her mind. That's not something that we're going to want to make a movie about, but... it's something that someone else can relate to."

Her solution directly reaches out to the women who feel they don't belong in the outdoors. Claire emphasized the importance of showing women that "the best skier on the mountain is the one who has the most fun... and the best woman in the outdoors is the one who has the most fun." In shaping this atmosphere in the outdoors, we'll "remove the barrier of 'okay I wanted to go hiking, but I can only go on these really basic small loops right outside of town, so since I can't get up on top of the mountain, I might as well not go.'"

I agreed with Claire when she said this. I hadn't realized it, but I often find myself replaying this internal dialogue of "If I can't go all the way, I might as well not go at all." It's difficult to get out into the "great outdoors" where I live in Washington, DC, but it's not necessarily difficult to go do something outside. For some reason, I feel like if I can't go see some great mountain or lake, I might as well skip the trip to the park down the block. If I can't do something great, I don't want to settle. It's just easier to do nothing at all.

This train of thought poses a big barrier to female participation in the outdoors. This barrier would surely break down if we worked to put Claire's solution into action. If we were able to succeed in altering the public dialogue to promote female athletes who get outdoors (even in the simplest ways) amidst their busy daily routine, we would create accessible inspiration. This in turn would lead more women to participate in the outdoors—at all levels.

* * *

Encouraging women to write for major outdoor news sources would also support change, according to Liz Thomas, a hiker most known for breaking the women's unsupported speed record (former) on the Appalachian Trail in 2011. She stated that women need to be presented as serious outdoor athletes instead of just bikinis on snowboards. "I remember ten years ago, a friend of mine wrote her thesis on portrayals of women in the outdoor media specifically citing how *Outside* magazine portrays female athletes," she said. "Now, it's ten years later, and *Outside* hasn't done much to have more articles focusing on women athletes/women's gear." These steps are important for us to consider, as they more broadly tackle the wide-spanning consequences that come from female objectification in the media.

"Getting more women outdoors and inspired and seeing female role models is a big part of changing the gender gap," she said. "But changing the media's portrayal of women—not just in women-centric outdoors news sources—but major outdoors news sources is something that really needs to change."

I heard a similar suggestion from long-distance runner and backpacker Kate Worteck. "I'd love to see female athletes getting equal shares of media coverage, sponsorship dollars, and gear options—that would be an incredible start," she said. "We're moving in that direction, but not as fast as I'd like."

Kate went on to say that she would also like to see more support for women-only backcountry trips. She stated that these trips are an enormous confidence booster, saying: "My friend Lauren and I did a seventy-mile loop through the Sierras earlier this summer, and in five days we saw only two other female-only groups. All of the other women we saw on the trail were with their boyfriends. And hiking with your boyfriend is great (I do it all the time!), but I think we're socialized to defer to men in those situations, and often dudes just naturally assume they'll be taking the role of trip planner, navigator, gear selector, etc. When you're forced to make all the decisions for yourself, you gain a lot of confidence, and you're more comfortable taking the lead on group trips."

* * *

Girl Ventures' Cori Coccia's suggestion had more to do with working on enlightening men. "More emphasis needs to be given to young men," she said. "I think that there needs to be more programs that have…depth and intentionality that work specifically with males." If more men in the world had exposure to a program such as the *Girl Venture* curriculum, there would be a lot more consciousness overall.

The girls in *Girl Ventures* are taught to identify who they are in the world and what their impact is and can be. "I think that if young men were guided through that curriculum as well, they could better understand sexism and issues of privilege from identifying who they are and what their impact is… and what that impact can be," Cori added. I really like that suggestion for change and think it would surely have a positive impact of gender bias within the Outdoor Industry.

Similar to *Girl Ventures,* Camber Outdoors is actively making the Outdoor Industry more accessible for women. The staff has made it their mission "to achieve equality for all women in the outdoors, from backcountry to boardroom. It is the only national organization dedicated to workplace diversity and inclusion by expanding opportunities for women and companies in the active-outdoor industries." They believe that making strides toward equality in the outdoors requires outdoor companies to actively recruit women to work in the industry.

Camber Outdoors has more than four thousand individual members and over 170 corporate partners. Seventy-five CEOs have made a commitment to "attracting, retaining, and advancing women in their workplaces," and these CEOs represent some of the biggest forces in the industry. Corporate bodies have much to gain from recruiting and retaining a diverse workforce, as "companies in the active-outdoor industries currently face competitive pressures in several areas, including: market share, profitability, sustainability, and sourcing, and companies employing a diverse workforce can supply a greater variety of solutions to these pressures because employees from varied backgrounds bring unique and fresh perspectives, ideas, and methodologies."[40]

Camber Outdoors is not only recruiting and providing opportunity for "athletes and mountain guides, but also accountants, IT specialists, educators, engineers and other professionals." Camber Outdoors is not only improving the female experience in the outdoors. They are building a healthier and more sustainable Outdoor Industry—as a diverse workforce leads

---

40 [i] "Advancing Women in Leadership: CEO Pledge." Camber Outdoors, camberoutdoors.org/ceo-pledge/.

to more innovative product design, which in turn leads to increased female participation in the outdoors. This new participation increases revenue flow into the Outdoor Sector.

In addition to the CEO pledge, Camber Outdoors puts together an annual pitchfest that features female entrepreneurs making waves in the Outdoor Industry. They also offer leadership webinars, mentoring resources, and networking opportunities. Additionally, they educate and inspire by putting on thought leader keynote events, and sharing stories of successful women in the Industry through their blog. Most notably, they have put together an extensive job board (accessed via their site) that includes hundreds of job postings from various outdoor companies. The Camber Outdoors team is taking a multifaceted approach to eliminating bias in the industry, and it is exciting to see the progress they are making.

* * *

Overall, there is no specific recipe for how to deal with gender bias in the outdoors, but thankfully, there are hundreds of men and women currently dedicating their lives to combatting the root causes of this bias. The one universal piece of advice I have gathered for the moment when an issue such as this arises is to remember your own self-worth and your capabilities. If it seems that addressing the bias directly would have an impact on the other people involved, and you feel comfortable doing so, do it! If it seems like addressing the bias directly would cause more harm than good, let yourself pass. If you don't feel comfortable doing so or fear directly addressing it would have negative personal consequences, it's okay to give yourself a break.

Many strong women and men are addressing the causes of gender bias on a large scale, and their efforts will bring change. I was really excited about these suggestions for improvement that came from the women I interviewed. I am looking forward to seeing these things take shape over my lifetime. After speaking with these incredibly inspirational and hard-working women, I am confident they will.

CONCLUSION

WE ARE THE
LUCKY ONES

———

"I think many women are just starting to realize that the out-doors is a place they can go and that they don't need a man to introduce them to the outdoors—they can go now. That's really powerful, especially for slightly older generations who may not have grown up believing this was a possibility."
—Liz Thomas, American long-distance adventure hiker

Our generation has untold potential. We have amazing women who have forged a path for us in the Outdoor Industry with their hard work and jaw-dropping accomplishments. More-over, we have access to numerous programs that have been created specifically with the intent to empower and include us in the outdoors.

These are a few strategic pieces of advice I have concluded from the women I spoke to:

Believe in yourself. You are far more capable than you think. The first and most important step in reaching your full potential is believing you can succeed.

Persevere in the face of bias. You can correct it, but don't have to. Ignorance exists, but is not a reflection on you in any way!

Open your eyes and ears. See and listen to the women who have showed us it can be done, and the women who have dedicated their lives to helping us get it done. We have a support system of strong women. Reach out to them, and ask questions.

Support other women. 'nuff said.

Surround yourself with people who support women. Some men empower women. Some do not. Some women empower women. Some do not. No matter how strong we are, life is easier when people around us believe in us.

Have courage in the outdoors. You belong there. You add value to the outdoors. You don't need to prove it and you don't need to be afraid of failing. It sounds cheesy to say failure makes us better, but it does. Make the leap, and take the risk. You will be better for it.

Don't settle. If you feel passionate about the outdoors, don't settle for a lifestyle that doesn't allow you to incorporate that passion into your daily routine. A passion for the outdoors doesn't mean you must necessarily work in the outdoors. Many women have jobs in different industries but still make time to enjoy outdoor activity.

Know that your path will take on an entirely unique form. There are hundreds of millions of ways to enjoy the outdoors and make a living. No woman has written the story you will write, and that's pretty exciting. Be prepared. You're about to make history, and that's not something to be afraid of. You are here to do just that.

APPENDIX

———

Staff, REI. "REI History: It Started With An Ice Axe." *REI Co-Op Journal*, REI, 6 Dec. 2016, www.rei.com/blog/camp/rei-history-it-started-with-an-ice-axe.

REI. "2017 National Study on Women and the Outdoors." *LinkedIn SlideShare*, REI, 30 Mar. 2017, www.slideshare.net/REI_/2017-national-study-on-women-and-the-outdoors.

REI. "Force of Nature." *REI*, www.rei.com/h/force-of-nature.

"Outdoor Participation Report 2016." *Outdoor Industry Association*, The Outdoor Foundation, outdoorindustry.org/resource/out-door-participation-report-2016/.

Chang, Angel. "Spending Time Outdoors Will Improve Your Health

In 9 Fascinating Ways." *LittleThings.com*, 17 Nov. 2015, www.
littlethings.com/benefits-of-being-outside/.

REI. "2017 National Study on Women and the Outdoors." *LinkedIn SlideShare*, REI, 30 Mar. 2017, www.slideshare.net/REI_/2017-national-study-on-women-and-the-outdoors.

"Interview: Elise Knicely // She Is ABLE | Misadventures." *Misadventures Magazine*, Misadventures, 17 May 2017, misadventuresmag.com/interview-elise-knicely-able/.

Malordy, Jessica C. "Traci Saor: Founder of G.O.N.E. | Misadventures." *Misadventures Magazine*, 19 Jan. 2017, misadventuresmag.com/traci-saor-founder-of-g-o-n-e/.

Malordy, Jessica C. "Traci Saor: Founder of G.O.N.E. | Misadventures." *Misadventures Magazine*, 19 Jan. 2017, misadventuresmag.com/traci-saor-founder-of-g-o-n-e/.

Johnstone, Lori, and Sydney Millar. "Actively Engaging Women and Girls." 2012.

Google Search, Google, www.google.com/search?ei=W2_mWvKSCsSxggfl84_YCA&q=definition%2Bof%2Binter-sectionality&oq=definition%2Bof%2Bintersection-ality&gs_l=psy-ab.3..0i67k1j0l5j0i22i10i30k1j0i22i30

k1l3.4481.4481.0.5056.1.1.0.0.0.0.67.67.1.1.0....0...1.1.64.
psy-ab..0.1.67....0.HG2gBP1NP40.

"Ambreen Tariq." *Diversify Outdoors*, www.diversifyoutdoors.com/
tariq.

"Adriana Garcia." *Diversify Outdoors*, www.diversifyoutdoors.com/
garcia.

Walker, Emma. "Diversity in the Outdoors: Why Does the Outdoor Industry (Still) Have a Diversity Problem?" *RootsRated
Media*, 11 July 2017, rootsrated.media/blog/the-outdoor-indus-
try-still-has-a-diversity-problem/.

Walker, Emma. "Diversity in the Outdoors: Why Does the Outdoor Industry (Still) Have a Diversity Problem?" *RootsRated
Media*, 11 July 2017, rootsrated.media/blog/the-outdoor-indus-
try-still-has-a-diversity-problem/.

"What Does It Mean to Be a Woman in the Outdoor Industry?" *Kim
Kircher*, 29 May 2015, kimkircher.com/2015/05/29/what-does-
it-mean-to-be-a-women-in-the-outdoor-industry/.

Crowther, Greg. "Gender and Endurance Performance." *Gender
and Endurance Performance*, faculty.washington.edu/crowther/
Misc/RBC/gender.shtml.

Press, The Associated. "Appalachian Record Set." *The New York Times*,
The New York Times, 13 July 2015, www.nytimes.com/2015/07/14/
sports/appalachian-record-set.html?mtrref=www.google.
com&gwh=8497BD86C33567FF99B8E12619E603C3&gwt=pay.

Plate, Katharine R. "Rock Climbing Is a Masculine Sport? Understanding the Complex Gendered Subculture of Rock Climbing.
." www.sheffield.ac.uk/polopoly_fs/1.71699!/file/10-Plate-article.
pdf.

"Sponsorship & Media." *Women In Sport*, www.womeninsport.org/
how-were-doing-it/sponsorship-media/.

Burakowski, Nina. "Why Kiteboarding Is for Girls." *Misadventures
Magazine*, misadventuresmag.com/why-kiteboarding-is-for-
girls/.

Bastone, Kelly. "We Need More Images of Women in Outdoor
Media." *Outside Online*, Outside Magazine, 11 Apr. 2017, www.
outsideonline.com/2172896/why-we-need REI. "2017 National
Study on Women and the Outdoors." *LinkedIn SlideShare*, REI,
30 Mar. 2017, www.slideshare.net/REI_/2017-national-study-
on-women-and-the-outdoors.

-women-outdoor-packaging.

Randall, Cassidy. "How Instagram Is Skewing the Way We Talk About

Women in the Outdoors." *Travel + Leisure*, www.travelandleisure.
com/trip-ideas/adventure-travel/women-adventurers.

"City Creep and the Perfect Outdoor Woman | Misadventures." *Misadventures Magazine*, 17 Dec. 2015, misadventuresmag.com/
city-creep-and-the-perfect-outdoor-woman/.

Barker, Sarah. "Empowering Women in the Outdoors: Why the
White-Hot Interest?" *Star Tribune*, Star Tribune, 29 June 2017,
www.startribune.com/women-in-the-outdoors-x2009-why-
all-the-white-hot-interest/431595953/.

Barker, Sarah. "Empowering Women in the Outdoors: Why the
White-Hot Interest?" *Star Tribune*, Star Tribune, 29 June 2017,
www.startribune.com/women-in-the-outdoors-x2009-why-
all-the-white-hot-interest/431595953/.

Barker, Sarah. "Empowering Women in the Outdoors: Why the
White-Hot Interest?" *Star Tribune*, Star Tribune, 29 June 2017,
www.startribune.com/women-in-the-outdoors-x2009-why-
all-the-white-hot-interest/431595953/.

Farnell, Shauna. "Elite Kayaker Adriene Levknecht's Drive Goes
Beyond The Boat." *ESPN*, ESPN Internet Ventures, 17 July 2015,
www.espn.com/espnw/athletes-life/article/13273576/elite-kay-
aker-adriene-levknecht-drive-goes-boat.

REI. "2017 National Study on Women and the Outdoors." *LinkedIn SlideShare*, REI, 30 Mar. 2017, www.slideshare.net/REI_/2017-national-study-on-women-and-the-outdoors.

REI. "2017 National Study on Women and the Outdoors." *LinkedIn SlideShare*, REI, 30 Mar. 2017, www.slideshare.net/REI_/2017-national-study-on-women-and-the-outdoors.

Chambers, Leah. "Interview: Christine Norton, Adventure Therapy Specialist." *Misadventures Magazine*, 9 Dec. 2015, misadventuresmag.com/interview-christine-norton-adventure-therapy-specialist/.

Lozancich, Katie. "How Nepali Women Find Freedom Through Mountain Biking." *Teton Gravity Research*, 6 Mar. 2018, www.tetongravity.com/video/bike/moksha-finding-freedom-and-empowerment-through-mountain-biking.

"The Power of Girls' Schools." *Girls Preparatory School | The Power of Girls' Schools*, www.gps.edu/page/why-a-girls-school/the-power-of-girls-schools.

"The Power of Girls' Schools." *Girls Preparatory School | The Power of Girls' Schools*, http://www.gps.edu/page/why-a-girls-school/the-power-of-girls-schools.

Wilson, Breanna. "How REI Mastered The Outdoor, Women-Only

Retreat." *Forbes*, Forbes Magazine, 19 Sept. 2017, www.forbes. com/sites/breannawilson/2017/09/19/how-rei-mastered-the-outdoor-women-only-retreat/#6bce019835fd.

Christensen, Megan. "'AndShesDopeToo' Empowering Women through Meetups, Clothing."*KSL.com*, www.ksl. com/?nid=1288&sid=36009839.

Megan. "ASDT Rendezvous." *The Quirky Climber*, 19 May 2017, thequirkyclimber.com/2016/09/15/asdt-rendezvous/.

Barker, Sarah. "Empowering Women in the Outdoors: Why the White-Hot Interest?"*Star Tribune*, Star Tribune, 29 June 2017, www.startribune.com/women-in-the-outdoors-x2009-why-all-the-white-hot-interest/431595953/.

Zulliger, Laura. "Women on Water." *Misadventures Magazine*, 20 Nov. 2015, misadventuresmag.com/women-on-water/.

"Advancing Women in Leadership: CEO Pledge." *Camber Outdoors*, camberoutdoors.org/ceo-pledge/.

Made in United States
North Haven, CT
24 June 2024

53997924R10111